What others have said...

"...a joy to read and a tremendous resource for helpful information as well."

I shared the *"Teacher Under Construction: Things I Wish I'd Known!"* book with my principal and she absolutely loved it too! She wants to order copies for some of our staff members. *(Francis Shroeder, Ph.D, Anaheim, CA)*

"This is practicality par excellence...a must for every new middle school teacher!"

Far removed from educational philosophy and pedantic educational theory, this little gem is a mine of practical teaching helps for new middle school teachers, drawn from the author's many years 'in the trenches'. A book is only as good as the author's understanding of his/her subject, and one has only to read "What is a Middle Schooler?" on page one to understand that this author knows what middle school is all about.

...make no mistake, this book is aimed squarely at new middle school teachers. It has been used in countless university educational prep courses, and while not of the scope of some more publicized tomes, it addresses every aspect of cogent information a new teacher should know... *(Dr. Elizabeth Delong, Horten Co. Schools)*

"A Must..."

I taught 7th grade for the first time last year as a veteran high school teacher and learned by trial and error some of the things discussed in this book. While experience is the best teacher, it was great to read it from someone who really knows what they are doing. A Must. *(Paul E., Brooklyn, NY)*

"A must-have gem for the new or initially licensed middle school teacher. Your pedagogy classes don't cover this..."

TOP PICK: If I'd had *Teacher Under Construction,* a book written specifically for middle school teachers, I suspect I would have gotten more sleep, fewer headaches, and organized my time more effectively. This book is a must-have gem for the new or initially licensed middle school teacher. Your pedagogy classes don't cover this stuff, and it seems that too few resources are dedicated to the squirrelly (but infinitely fun) middle schooler. *(TOP FIVE **AvantGarde** Teacher Review)*

D1512074

Teacher Under Construction: Things I Wish I'd Known

Teacher Under Construction: Things I Wish I'd Known!

A Survival Handbook for New Middle School Teachers

Ten Critical Building Blocks for Success Every New Middle School Teacher Should Know the First Year

Jerry L. Parks, Ed.S, NBCT

iUniverse, Inc.
New York   Bloomington

Teacher Under Construction: Things I Wish I'd Known!

iUniverse books may be ordered through booksellers or by contacting:

iUniverse
1663 Liberty Drive
Bloomington, IN 47403
www.iuniverse.com
1-800-Authors (1-800-288-4677)

Because of the dynamic nature of the Internet, any Web addresses or links contained in this book may have changed since publication and may no longer be valid. The views expressed in this work are solely those of the author and do not necessarily reflect the views of the publisher, and the publisher hereby disclaims any responsibility for them.

ISBN: 978-1-4502-4426-8 (sc)
ISBN: 978-1-4502-4427-5 (ebook)

Printed in the United States of America

iUniverse rev. date: 07/29/2010

About the Author

Jerry Parks earned a B.S., M.A., & Ed.S degrees in Education from Eastern Kentucky University, and completed additional graduate work at the University of Kentucky. He is a *Nationally Board Certified Teacher*, a member of the *USA-TODAY All-American Teacher Team*, and a member of the *National Teachers Hall of Fame*. He has received numerous "Teacher of the Year" honors at the local, state, and national level. He is a regular speaker at the *National Middle School Association* conferences, and is currently an instructor of social studies at Georgetown Middle School in Georgetown, Kentucky. Dr. Parks has several previously published books, including:

"So, You Want to be an NBPTS Certified Teacher?", a handbook for teachers considering the National Board Certification Process

"So, You Want to be an NBPTS Certified Teacher: Workbook & Evidence Manual", a step-by-step, hands-on workbook to assist candidates in completing the *NBPTS* process

"Mentoring the NBPTS Candidate", a handbook for mentors of the National Board Certification Process

"Help! My Child is Starting Middle School!", a guide for parents of soon-to-be middle schoolers

"A Gilgamesh Play for Teen Readers", a short play for middle and high schools classrooms, based upon the story of Gilgamesh and the culture of ancient Sumer

"With Joseph in the University of Adversity: The Mizraim Principles", a study of the life of the Old Testament hero, Joseph

"God, Help Me Pray!", and *"God, Help Me Pray!: Workbook and Journal"*, teachings on prayer from a Biblical perspective

"Dragons, Grasshoppers, & Frogs!", a handbook for teenagers and new Christians on the Book of Revelation

Dr. Parks is available for speaking engagements at schools and conferences. He can be reached via e-mail at: *kidztchr7@hotmail.com.*

Foreword

Over the past decade, I have had the privilege of assigning many aspiring and committed education majors to the classroom of Dr. Jerry Parks. Each semester I have enjoyed saying, without reservation, that Dr. Parks wrote the book on middle school education and indeed he has! Since its original printing six years ago, no other book has captured the magic and mystery of the modern-day middle-school student, like *Teacher Under Construction.*

Based on his years of experience in the middle grades classroom, Dr. Parks has skillfully taken pen to paper or fingers to keyboard, and insightfully demonstrated his passion and philosophy by sharing his observations and experiences with those complicated kids known as 'tweens'. For those of us who have followed other teaching levels, it is difficult to understand the driving force behind choosing to go into a 6th, 7th or 8th grade classroom when there are clearly other teaching options. However, as evidenced in his book, Dr. Jerry Parks has taken a "road less traveled" and he has "…made all the difference."

Despite all the disintegrating forces of life, *Teacher Under Construction* serves as a guide to the joys and challenges present in the daily teaching of middle schoolers. From his "aha" moment describing a student's decorated locker of pictures of puppies and heart-throbs, to user-friendly lists of "do's and don'ts", Dr. Parks reminds the reader of the importance of taking time to listen with interest to students, and work to not just learn their names, but their needs.

More than a handbook, *Teacher Under Construction* focuses on the power of a positive self-image through classroom esprit de corps. Engaging students, faculty and family through collaboration, Dr. Parks suggests strategies for affirming and "lifting up" students, individually and collectively.

Whether you are an elementary, middle, secondary, or collegiate educator or a parent of a middle school student, you will find yourself consistently reaching for *Teacher Under Construction* for inspiration and personal affirmation. Because it is interwoven with threads of insightfulness, passion and commitment necessary for guiding these lifelong learners toward their individual goals and achievements, I can say that not only does Jerry Parks embrace the principles and precepts of middle school education, but he wrote the book.

Carol Williams
Assistant Professor of Education
Georgetown College
Georgetown, KY

Contents

Principle—"The first step in becoming a professional is *presenting* yourself as one!"

Lesson I must learn: Your professionalism will be seen in everything you do and say within your classroom. Be sure you take your professionalism seriously. The impressions you make on other teachers, parents, and students will be lasting ones. Make them positive!

> ➢ Appearances are everything
> ➢ The *'attitude challenge!'*
> ➢ The Nike Factor: *'Growing Pro'*
> ➢ The lesson from the cow
> ➢ Your most important Latin lesson!

Principle— "A good teacher teaches *students* the subject, not the *subject* to students!"

Lesson I must learn: The more efficiently your classroom learning environment functions, the greater success you will have in promoting student achievement. Create a classroom where your students *want* to learn and *enjoy* coming to class. If you can do this, you will smooth the road to successful learning!

> ➢ Discipline by design!
> ➢ Expectations
> ➢ Anticipation: Closing the loopholes!
> ➢ Celebrating achievement: *Rewards*
> ➢ When all else fails…

> The 3 'R's'
> Homework
> The Socrates Effect
> Assessment

6. Attitudes: *Building Atmosphere—creating a magical environment!*

Principle—"As a teacher, your job is not to fill a bucket, but to light a fire!"

Lesson I must learn: Your attitude toward your subject and your students is the most important key to student achievement. Your students will often learn more from the fire of your presentation than from the information in your lesson. Be excited! Enjoy what you do!

> Attitude Creates Atmosphere
> The P.I.E. of Successful Teaching
> Inviting Room or Grant's Tomb?
> Descending the ivory tower

7. Strategies: *Building Learning—strategies that make it work!*

Principle—"Learning should be enjoyable! Make sure you don't kill their hearts by pounding their heads!"

Lesson I must learn: There is no perfect way to teach a lesson. It is the diversity in teaching strategies that make every classroom unique. However, a few strategies have stood the test of time, and are universally helpful in making students enjoy—not merely endure—the learning experience. Utilize and modify what has worked in the past to create new and innovative ways to teach your subject!

> *Numero Uno* on their list!
> Empowering your students—the fuel that runs their engines!
> The *'5-10-15-20'* rule!
> Teachable Moments
> Lay down a challenge
> Cooperative Learning
> Shock their socks off!
> *'Dead Poets'* DO speak!

Principle—"The broader the foundation, the taller the construction!"

Lesson I must learn: Working with other teachers in a team setting can greatly improve not only your effectiveness as a teacher, but also the ability of your students to broaden their learning experience. Use the leverage of interdisciplinary teaming to make your students multidimensional learners!

> ➢ Fitting In, and Firing Up
> ➢ Together—*we can!*
> ➢ Collaboration

Principle—"A teacher can never understand what motivates a student at school until he/she understands the 'hidden rules' in which that student was raised at home."

Lesson I must learn: The economic diversity of the students in your classroom is based upon patterns of unspoken clues and habits extant at home. Understanding these patterns and teaching expectations will enable your students to become more successful at school, and in the middle school social environment.

> ➢ What Ruby Payne's Framework is *not*
> ➢ Motivational and driving forces of your students
> ➢ Managing behaviors
> ➢ Successful strategies

Principle—"It is better to learn from the mistakes and the wisdom of others than to learn from your own mistakes over time."

Lesson I must learn: Picking the brain of numerous successful teachers with decades of middle school experience can save you infinite time and heartache. Here are lessons from experience—as well as general tips—to make your first year a more successful year!

> ➢ "What I wish the experts had told me my first year of teaching…."

Appendices: Handouts and Supplementary helps 82

Preface to the Second Edition

It has been nearly six years since the publication of the first edition of *Teacher Under Construction*. From the many positive reviews and comments made to me by numerous beginning teachers, the book has served its purpose as intended.

Nevertheless, due to the many suggestions offered to me at conferences, schools, and from individual colleagues whose opinion I sincerely value, I feel it is time for a revision.

This second edition includes further research, additional websites, the inclusion of Ruby Payne's study on how teachers should address economic diversity, as well as a chapter offering over one-hundred-sixty of the finest tips from some of the best teachers in America.

Most of the material remains unchanged. The information is just as appropriate now as it was six years ago. In my classroom a poster reads: *"It's not true because I tell you; I tell you because it's true."* I can say the same for the information and the suggestions in this book. It is hoped that *Teacher Under Construction* will continue to help new teachers become the best they can be as they hone their skills during that most amazing first year.

Jerry Parks
Author

Preface

"The entrance to the student's mind is though the child's heart."

Jessica ran into my room one morning, bubbling with excitement! "Come see my locker!" she urged, while spilling a half dozen gummy bears upon my recently organized desk. "I've decorated!"

Obligingly, I followed the precocious twelve-year-old into the hall. As she opened her locker for me to behold, Jessica beamed with pride. An unremarkable metal-encased hole in a wall had now been wonderfully transformed into the home away from home for her belongings for the next 180 days. As I marveled at Jessica's masterpiece of décor, I glimpsed, on the inside of her locker door, a photograph of the cutest collection of puppies I had ever seen. 'So typical,' I thought to myself, 'of what would win the heart of a little girl. How cute!'

Suddenly, my eyes glanced to the interior of Jessica's locker. Lovingly taped to the back wall was the full-body pin-up of the latest teen idol, scantily clad, and enticing in appearance. It was then that it hit me—*this* is what a middle schooler is! Random motion, jumbled chaos, and predictable unpredictability—a child becoming an adult—paused for one magical moment between puppies and sex symbols, and running on hormones and gum, with engines that somehow seem to never run out of gas.

As a new middle school teacher, you are about to embark upon the most wonderful and challenging career you could ever have chosen! You will make mistakes along your journey, but do not get discouraged. Middle school is world of pencils—and *erasers*. Never forget that. You will often be told that teaching middle schoolers is the most difficult teaching assignment of all. Perhaps it is. But if you are willing to put forth the hard work that teaching this age-level requires, you will find working with middle schoolers the most rewarding daily experience on Planet Earth! *Teacher Under Construction: Things I Wish I'd Known!* is merely an effort to get you started off on the right foot.

Lesson One. There are no immediate heroes in teaching. You will not walk in and become 'Teacher of the Year'. Establishing a reputation, developing an *effective* behavior management plan, building rapport with the families of your students in the community—all these take time, and sometimes a *long* time. Be patient and grow. This is Lesson One.

Lesson Two. You are selling a product called education. Make it palatable. To do so effectively you will need to be a magician, an actor, a storyteller, a wizard, an artist, a politician, a philosopher, a salesperson and a psychologist. Whatever it takes—sell to your audience.

In her excellent work *The Truth About Teaching*[1], Coleen Armstrong wisely points out that you will give your heart to middle schoolers, and they will both break it, and at the same time, fill it with joy. She also posits that teachers meet only eight students in a teaching career: the rebel, the brain, the delinquent, the bully, the recluse, the queen bee, the misunderstood genius, and the class clown. Although I would add: the eccentric, she is probably right. In this book, I will attempt to help you learn how to teach all of these.

If an expert is an ordinary person who attempts extraordinary feats, I truly qualify. Not because this book presents concepts that are new or profound, but because for *any* individual to presume to have empirically correct answers as to what makes the perfect middle teacher is as *extraordinary* as it is *impossible*.

This book is not intended to be a compendium of teaching strategies, research, or procedures. There are many books available for these. *Teacher Under Construction: Things I Wish I'd Known!* is only intended to be a ready-reference basic training manual to equip newer middle school teachers with enough information to survive the first year of middle school. It is merely a jump-start guide to support the novice instructor until he or she can formulate personal paradigms of what works and what doesn't. Much of the information will be relevant across the curriculum. Other information is gleaned from twenty years of personal experience in the social studies classroom. All of the information is suitable to personal adaptation, and is presented in light of pragmatic practicality rather than exhaustive research.

It is said that 'teachers are born with the talent, but *good* teachers are made by the experience.' One purpose of this book is to allow talented teachers to *become* good teachers. Research tells us that 14% of new teachers quit after the first year, and less than 46% of new teachers will remain in the classroom after five years[2]. Only in seeing the profession as a satisfying and enjoyable environment can talented teachers develop the experiences that make a successful middle school teacher. Experienced teachers, on the other hand, may recognize within these pages much of what they already do, for time has a way of quickly refining, for every teacher, what will and won't work in a middle school classroom.

The information and suggestions found within these pages are the culmination of many years of presenting at conferences across the country, including regular sessions at the *National Middle School Association* national convention. They reflect my personal philosophy in dealing with middle schoolers. Although most have been validated by research, they are not intended to be paradigms of the latest and greatest methodology in our field.

It is hoped that you—the new middle school teacher—will be able to utilize, refine, and modify the information presented in this book, and in doing so, avoid many of the pitfalls that line the paths of inexperience in the middle school classroom. The suggestions and teaching strategies do not work because I offer them. I offer them because they work.

I would like to thank the thousands of teenagers who have surrendered one year of their lives to be my students at *Tates Creek Middle School* in Lexington, KY, and *Georgetown Middle School*, in Georgetown, KY. Without their patience, and the support and contributions of innumerable professional peers with whom I've had the pleasure to work, this book would not have been possible.

Jerry L. Parks, NBCT
Georgetown Middle School
Email: *Kidztchr7@hotmail.com*

Introduction

Congratulations—you've become a teacher. Kudos—you're a middle school teacher! You are about to enter the strange and wonderful world of middle schoolers. They will delight you, and they will frustrate you. They will both boost and deflate your ego, and for the most part, leave you exhausted yet satisfied at the end of each day. In addition to the information contained elsewhere in this book (See Appendix E: *Characteristics & Needs of Middle Schoolers*), let's get to know the young people you are about to meet, teach and influence on a daily basis.

- Middle schoolers have bodies which sometimes seem foreign to its inhabitants.

- Middle schoolers see the word 'organization' as a term forever in search of a definition.

- Middle schoolers' concepts of values and morality are cast upon the testing block.

- Middle schoolers' independence from their parents is matched only by their dependence on the opinions of their peers.

- Middle schoolers identify with the popular and gravitate to the bizarre.

- Middle schoolers' desire for individual praise is inversely proportioned to their ability to handle it in front of their friends.

- Middle schoolers' inquisitiveness is only matched by their ability to surprise through creativity if only given the chance.

Middle schoolers develop in ways in which they will never develop again. Sixth grade is a time of great change in the adolescent brain. This is the year children become better able to move from the concrete thoughts into the abstract world of theory and possibility. They learn *empathy*, not just sympathy, and their concept of the world grows by leaps and bounds. Children become able to think of the world, issues, and concepts in a more global perspective. They begin to understand that there is more to living in the world than they have encountered to this point in their lives, and that other people's realities are different from theirs, and will influence the way they think and act.

Brain development in seventh graders causes them to develop further independence and self-expression. Irrationality and emotional upheaval can cause them to no longer be the child they were in earlier grades. They reach for anything and grab for everything. Seventh graders begin to settle into the new realities they discovered in the sixth grade.

Eighth grade, while a somewhat less chaotic period, is a time of strengthening relationships, and a time when what parents say begins to have an even lessening impact. By this point, middle schoolers are becoming less children, and are rapidly transforming into the young adults they are going to grow up to be.

Middle schoolers' brains actually map new ways of thinking and grow in capacity. This is the time period of rapid growth in their physical and mental worlds. Because of this, they may not always think logically, or even clearly, but they're doing the best they can. Your job is to help them get through this time, so they can grow and become the best people they can possibly be.

The purpose of this book is to offer simple, everyday, practical help to you, the new middle school teacher. This book is intended to be a personalized, conversational (excuse repetition, and often excessive use of italics) handbook on the holistic—not merely academic—teaching of middle schoolers. Any new middle school teacher seeking only to put in an 8-3 workday teaching academics alone—having little concern with lessons of modeling, character, and making middle schoolers actually enjoy the world of learning—will glean little from this book. This book is written for teachers of young people, not mere conduits of information. You can certainly be a good teacher without practicing all the suggestions in this book. But you will be a *better* teacher if you will at least take the time to consider them.

What is a Middle Schooler?

By J. L. Parks

A middle schooler is random motion, jumbled chaos, and predictable unpredictability—a child becoming an adult—paused for one magical moment between pictures of puppies, and pin-ups of sex symbols. They are a walking paradox of fashionless style, fueled by hormones and gum, and fired by engines that seem to never run out of gas. They are strongly independent social creatures that travel in packs and communicate by sacred note. They are nourished by the immediate, unencumbered by past, and impatient for the tomorrow they feel will never come.

Middle schoolers can miss the obvious, harp on the obscure, and defend the impossible. They thrive on spontaneity, loathe predictability, and refuse to even acknowledge the parents they love. They deny the proven, dispute the certain, stand up for the irrelevant, and fall out of chairs. Tapping is their anthem, and fairness—their rule of life. They are possessed of selective memory, and a fierce loyalty to their own kind. Their hair is their banner, disorder—their creed. Their image is the only thing that matters more than lunch.

Middle schoolers are bolts of energy wrapped in a package of laziness. They are confusion poured into mood swings—fueled by encouragement, motivated by curiosity, and stimulated by challenge. They are inspired by sincerity, frustrated by denial, and defeated by doubt. They are gangly growth spurts with a twinkle in their eyes. They are confident pretenders masquerading in fragile shells of insecurity—trusting skeptics—secretly searching for heroes.

Middle schoolers love to be hugged, but hate to be touched. They are reactive agents who cling to routine while reaching for change. They are reminders of our own immortality; in-progress paradigms of possibility in whose lives we plant a lesson, shape a behavior, mold a character, and seal a destiny. They are the first blooms of tomorrow's hope—fleeting sunbeams of a thirteenth springtime—on loan to a winter world.

1. Professionalism: *Building a Teacher— finding the professional within you!*

Principle—*"The first step in becoming a professional is presenting yourself as one!"*

Lesson I must learn: Your professionalism will be seen in everything you do and say within your classroom. Be sure you take your professionalism seriously. The impressions you make on other teachers, parents, and students will be lasting ones. Make them positive!

> ➤ Appearances are everything
> ➤ The *'attitude challenge!'*
> ➤ The Nike Factor: *'Growing Pro'*
> ➤ The lesson from the cow
> ➤ Your most important Latin lesson!

Appearances are everything

When I spent time selling real estate, one of the first things I was told was the importance of my attire. Dressing nicely served a twofold purpose. First, it created a professional appearance for those with whom I dealt. Second, it made me *feel* professional, and made it easier for me to perform as one.

As a teacher, it may not be practical to wear a coat and tie, or dress clothing to school. Neither is it professional to dress like the students you will teach. Strive to achieve the happy medium. Unless your school has a dress code for teachers, dress comfortably enough to do your job effectively, yet nicely enough to be seen as the professional you are. (Comfortable shoes are *especially* important.) Make no mistake— the way you dress in your classroom affects the respect your students will have for you, and the authority they perceive you to possess. The professional world has long known that we perform more effectively if we dress more professionally. Balance comfort and appearance. Never forget, however, you are *not* the age of your students. Don't try to dress like them.

Your personal appearance is only part of your professionalism. The appearance of your room, grade book, and planning book also tells a story. Keep your classroom looking as though your students were coming in—not as though they had already been there. Balance a creative and exciting classroom appearance with a clean and inviting atmosphere. Keep your grade book organized. Write out lesson plans, and keep your planning book such that the substitute can read and understand it. Days will come when they will need to.

While all aspects of how you present yourself are vital, the most important part of your appearance is your vocabulary. Not only your students, but also the peers and parents you work with every day, will evaluate you by the words that come out of your mouth. You are a communicator by profession—learn how to speak correctly. If you can't speak with a teacher's authority, you will have difficulty inspiring confidence in your students and your peers.

Many years ago, I attended a national conference for educators and looked forward to a session led by one of the premier writers in the field. I went to the session early, and, because so many others were excited to hear this presenter, I found it difficult to find a seat. Squeezed in on the back row, I waited—pen in hand—for the pearls of wisdom I was sure would make me a better teacher. The speaker began by offering helpful information on classroom management, but as he continued, I noticed how often he managed to butcher the English language. Soon, I found myself noting the speaker's language and diction rather than his content. Not only was it unpleasant to listen to, but the poor diction and improperly spoken English reduced the confidence I had in the speaker.

> There is one lesson you teach every day to every student. Modeling proper behavior.

Excelling as a public speaker is not a prerequisite for being a good teacher. Using correct diction (and *spelling!*), however, and correctly mastering the English language, is! You *will* make an impression—one way or another—by the vocabulary that comes out of your mouth. Even if you cannot speak *professionally*, learn to speak *correctly*. Your students who must listen to you deserve no less. The way you speak not only creates an appearance, it inspires confidence.

The way you allow your students to speak to you also affects your professionalism. Never allow them to call you by your first name, or simply by your last name alone. Insist that they be respectful enough to address you with 'Mr.', 'Ms.', Mrs.' or 'Dr.' You've been where they are, but they've never been in your position. Demand respect.

Finally, it should go without saying that the subject of your conversations at school should always be appropriate for the environment in which you work. While the kids may think you're cool by adopting their language, or laughing at questionable jokes, remember, *you* are the professional. You will gain no lasting respect by talking like your students. Be careful what you say around them. Be an *example* of what you'd like them to be—not a *buddy* who speaks their lingo. Your students need a *mentor*—not a 'teacher best friend'. If you don't remember that, you'll soon find yourself being worked by the crowd. Too, never forget, you are always being evaluated by the words that come out of your mouth. You are a professional—act like one.

The 'Attitude Challenge!'

There are three very contagious entities in a middle school classroom: boredom, apathy, and enthusiasm. Propagate the last, and the first two will cease to exist. *Attitude*, that is, how you feel about your subject and job, *creates* atmosphere. If your students know you love what you do, and genuinely care about them, you

> Remember the 'Law of Teaching Triangulation': If you care about your students, and you care about your subject, you can get your students to care about your subject!

will create an atmosphere where learning takes place. In middle school, the old maxim is never truer: students don't care how much you know until they know how much you care—about them, your subject, your job.

Maya Angelou once said: "They may forget what you said, and they may forget what you did, but they will always remember how you made them feel." This is ever so true with middle schoolers.

Here is a challenge I often make to new teachers. I have yet to have one tell me it doesn't work. Show your students you love your subject, make them feel you also love them, and your students will love your class!

The Nike factor: 'Growing Pro'

Nike was the Greek goddess of victory. In recent commercials, the Nike Company employed a catchphrase, *'Just do it!'* Such an edict is sometimes required for us as teachers because of our reticence to perform activities that seem to reside just outside the realm of importance. Such activities are important, however, and will make you more familiar with your subject, enable you to create more effective lesson plans, and improve your standing in the education profession. Considering these as priorities right now may not seem as important as teaching your students, but as Nike says—*just do it*!

First, join your state and national associations. It's good policy as a teaching professional. These organizations can offer you legal assistance, liability insurance, and professional development opportunities, as well as helpful publications and discounts.

Second, attend—and consider presenting at—*NMSA* and your subject area conferences. You can do this solo or as part of your team. Conferencing is the one single most effective professional development you can do. Let me repeat—*this is the one single most effective professional development you can do.* In attending these, you are learning from your peers—teachers just like you. You will return with innovative and successfully proven teaching ideas, become aware of the latest strategies and research in your field, and be able to share information with others who can learn from *you*. Apply and check funds early—these conferences are highlights of the school year.

Third, read the literature in your field. Subscribe to a journal. Be aware of the latest research. Learn how to utilize the Educational Research Information Center (ERIC). Grow *better* in what you do—not just older.

Fourth, learn how to network. Get 'in the loop' or 'on the grapevine' of what's taking place in education. Join or organize a support group. Volunteer for county and state committees involving curriculum, textbooks, and testing. Communicate with others in your field. Learn from them. Allow them to learn from you. Join teacher chat rooms on the Internet, and keep abreast of what others in your subject area are doing that really *works*.

Fifth, present yourself as a professional. Create a business card to pass out at conferences, or wherever you may want to let other professionals know you are proud to be an educator! Cards can be designed online inexpensively, and should reflect you as a teacher. Be creative! Include a short but memorable quote, or personal philosophy of teaching. Don't forget to include your school email. A business card makes you look professional and comes in handy at conferences and parent meetings.

Sixth, keep an ongoing personal portfolio. You are growing as a professional and should document your accomplishments along the way. Keep letters from parents and the community as well as touching notes from students. (See Appendix T: *Important Documents to Keep!*) Keep an updated resume. Catalogue your evaluations and professional development. These will come in handy when you least expect it and will prove invaluable should you seek *National Board Certification* in the future.

Seventh, recognize your limits. Learn how to say *no* sometimes—you can't do everything. For example, don't attempt to sponsor clubs and organizations until you become comfortable with your role as teacher. Don't frustrate yourself trying to accomplish the impossible. Set goals, but set *realistic* goals. Learn to prioritize. Conserve your energy. Find a hobby. Recognize that there is no shame in putting aside the business of school for a while.

Eighth, whether in an official or unofficial capacity, seek out and learn from a mentor. Experienced (and retired) teachers have much to offer and can share advice that will save you time, frustration, and difficulty in every aspect of your job as teacher. A good mentor should be in your teaching area and share your planning period if at all possible. Mentors can observe and evaluate you, remind you of important concerns, serve you as an advocate, and encourage you when things get tough. Such teachers will not seek you out. Find them, sit in on their classes and take notes—pick their brains, and do not perceive them as professionals from a bygone era. Really listen to your mentor but do not copy them. Understanding their wisdom will make you a better teacher.

Finally, never make big—possibly life-changing—decisions your first year of teaching. This is a stressful and challenging job at best, and not the time to make career choices you might possibly regret later. Realize that your first years are the most difficult of all, and that big decisions are better made when you are settled into a career rather than when you are simply trying to establish one.

The lesson from the cow

I once heard a story about an old country preacher who got all his sermon material from the sermons of other preachers. He was often seen copying sermon illustrations from radio ministers and carefully noting various tidbits from every evangelist that came to his city. Finally, one of his parishioners approached him to ask why he thought it necessary to copy every other minister's material instead of coming up with his own. *"Why, it's a lesson I learned from my cow"*, the preacher responded. *"She grazes on many pastures, but she gives her own milk."*

Learn from many sources, and modify their ideas to suit your own style. Watch experienced teachers—sit in on their classes during a planning period. Consider suggestions and recommendations on your evaluations. Read the latest research. When you have seen what others do or recommend, modify it to your teaching style, your students, and your subject area—and see if it works.

Your most important Latin lesson!

A final way that you exhibit professionalism is in your relationship to your students, and this is the most important relationship of all.

In loco parentis. The most important Latin lesson you, as a professional educator, will ever learn. *In loco parentis*—'in the position or place of a parent.' This is your legal status regarding the lives entrusted to your care, and you'd better never—*ever*—forget it.

As a teacher, you are held legally responsible for every word you say and every action you take regarding the children you teach. You are expected to know what is—and is not—appropriate in a public school classroom. This is more than just an important responsibility—it's the law. Ignorance is no excuse. You'd better take special care what you say or do regarding your students. Think long and hard before you tell that crude or questionable joke. Remember your audience.

Do not allow yourself to compromise—or be compromised—in your status as a professional educator. For example, never—*ever* show inappropriate films in your classroom. If there is a question at all regarding videos, have an administrator preview them with you and/or send home a permission slip.

Also, think carefully before you take a student home in your car, put your hands on a student, or allow yourself to be alone for an extended period with a student of the opposite sex. Consider carefully what books you assign for reading, what pictures you show, and—above all—what language you use in front of impressionable middle schoolers. Countless careers have been clouded by one unwise choice made in a school classroom. Innumerable reputations have been ruined by teachers who allowed themselves to be put into a compromising situation. *You are establishing a reputation with students and their families that will follow you for many years. Do not damage it with unwise actions.* What students may initially think makes you 'cool' can eventually damage your reputation and will never earn you lasting respect as a teacher. Regarding what you say or do around your students, a good rule of thumb to remember is: when in doubt—*don't*.

In loco parentis. The most important Latin lesson you will ever learn.

The least I need to know: My to do checklist!

- ❑ I will remember that I will *first* be judged by my appearance, and my abilities afterward.

- ❑ I will remember that after my appearance, the next things I will be judged by are the words that come out of my mouth.

- ❑ I will remember to insist that my students address me by name in a respectful manner.

- ❏ I will balance professional dress with comfort.

- ❏ I will remember that organization is paramount, and there is a direct relationship between organization and effectiveness as a teacher.

- ❏ I will remember that students generally rise to the level of expectation set for them.

- ❏ I will remember that the three most contagious entities in middle school are boredom, apathy, and enthusiasm.

- ❏ I will remember that my students don't care how much I know until they know how much I care—about them, and my job.

- ❏ I will remember that I am a professional, and a lifelong learner, and that learning began—but did not end—with my hire.

- ❏ I will get involved with professional organizations and committees within my school system and the state.

- ❏ I will seek out a mentor, and keep and update a personal portfolio.

- ❏ I will make sure I have a life outside of school with hobbies, interests and friends.

- ❏ I will attend meetings and conferences for my subject area as often as I am able.

- ❏ I will learn from others, and modify to suit my students and subject area.

- ❏ I will *never* allow myself to be put in compromising situations with my students.

- ❏ I will never forget: 'When in doubt—*don't!*'

2. Structure: *Building a Classroom—*
the foundation &
fabric of learning!

Principle— *"A good teacher teaches students the subject, not the subject to students!"*

Lesson I must learn: The more efficiently your classroom learning environment functions, the greater success you will have in promoting student achievement. Create a classroom where your students *want* to learn and *enjoy* coming to class. If you can do this, you will smooth the road to successful learning!

> ➤ Discipline by design!
> ➤ Expectations
> ➤ Anticipation: Closing the loopholes!
> ➤ Celebrating achievement: *Rewards*
> ➤ When all else fails…

"Peace is not the absence of conflict, but the ability to cope with conflict through peaceful means."
—*President Ronald Reagan*

Discipline by design!

Your students come first. As a teacher, in everything you do, remember—your students come *first*.

Never forget that middle schoolers are children—*not* little adults—and children very often see behavior management differently from you.

Before we discuss this topic, it is important to define some terms regarding discipline. Understanding these will cast a different light on how you may choose to handle problems in your classroom. Doug Lemov[3] has defined the terms in the following way:

Discipline—what and how you want your students to do
things
Management—the consequences and rewards of infractions
and actions

Control—how well students do what is asked, regardless of consequences
Influence—inspiring the desire to be successful
Engagement—how thoroughly your students are on task and lost in their work

Your discipline policy will be dependent on how well you <u>manage</u> and <u>control</u> your students through influence and engagement.

Middle schoolers tend to see the classroom as a democracy. It is actually a *benevolent dictatorship*. While students should be involved to some degree in the decision-making process, never let them forget that *you* are the one in charge. Establish your discipline policy on Day One. Until you establish a comfortable relationship with your students, you should begin tough, and ease up later. *The opposite approach is virtually impossible.*

> **Establish your discipline code early and take the first opportunity to enforce it. The atmosphere you establish in your classroom during the first two weeks will determine 90% of how your classroom functions for the rest of the year.**

Basically, there are two philosophies on discipline. You can discipline through fear and intimidation (active management), or through kindness, concern, and encouragement (passive management). While the first approach is more immediately effective, the second will be more constructive—for you and your students—over time. Concern and encouragement are necessary staples in a classroom anyway. Fear and intimidation are not, and will eventually wear thin in their effectiveness. Strive for passive management with your middle schoolers. Active management may be sprinkled in as necessary, but remember—like a good flavoring—a little goes a long way. Vanilla extract makes everything taste better, but alone is quite bitter. Reserve active management for occasions when all else has failed.

Whatever type of discipline policy you choose to employ, make sure it is *clear, concise,* and *consistent.* If your students do not fully understand your expectations, you will create only confusion. If your expectations are complicated, your discipline policy will cause frustration and destroy the atmosphere of order you are trying to create. If you are inconsistent in enforcing your expectations,

> **Atmosphere is your first and most important creation. Middle schoolers thrive on challenge, but freeze on threat. Remember, if the tone is pleasant, you can be off-key a few times, and the song will still be remembered!**

students will not take your policy seriously. However, if students know your expectations and understand the value of cooperating with those expectations, you will succeed at behavior management.[4]

First, decide if the unwanted behavior is *defiance* or *non-compliance*. Defiance is active, verbal, or physical resistance to instructions, directions, requests or demands. Non-compliant behavior is more indirect and passive. It might include complaining, whining, delaying, ignoring requests, crying, or ignoring others.[5] Defiance is a more serious offense, and should be dealt with in a different manner.

Second, make sure your behavior management policy is *clear*. What is it you want? Make a list of desired behaviors and state clearly the behavior you expect your students to model. Set high expectations, and praise positive behavior. Give them a *chance* to be good. Be specific. Give the relevant information your students will need in order to meet your specific expectations. Never forget—if you expect it, *teach it*. You might even allow students to have some measure of input regarding the policies, but, whether or not you do this, you will find your policies to be more effective if they are clearly posted somewhere in your room. Clear expectations are also stated *specifically*. For example, say to your students, *"Bring to class your notebook and writing materials,"* instead of *"Come prepared for class."* Stating your behavior management policies in a positive, rather than negative, manner is also more effective. For example, say to your students, *"Let ME dismiss you when the bell rings, and you will have more travel time,"* instead of *"Don't jump up when the bell rings, or you will have to sit back down."* Remember that instructions are clear only if your students' *perspectives* are clear!

> Never be afraid to be honest, and say, "I don't know." Middle schoolers appreciate sincerity.

During my first year of teaching, one of my lunch period students was experiencing behavior management difficulties in the cafeteria. When I could deal with it no more, I implored him to *"...behave in the lunchroom as you would behave in a restaurant!"* Sometime later, I saw the student with his parents at McDonald's and came to realize the way he had behaved in the cafeteria *was* the way he behaved in a restaurant! My expectation carried no challenge for the student since—through *his* perspective—his behavior was acceptable. Always remember that your perspective—and the perspective of your students—may not always be the same!

Clarity of your discipline policy is also dependent on the *relevancy* of that policy. Be sure your students see the objectives or the relevancy in the desired behavior you seek to teach. In discussing desired behaviors with your students, ask them, *"Why is this important?"* Be sure they *understand* the importance—and the consequences of your policy. In this way, you can be sure they know the *reasoning* for your discipline policy. This better enables them to 'buy into' the policy, since they know its significance and relevance.

Clarity is also dependant on *understanding*—be sure students are clear on your classroom expectations. Say what you mean—mean what you say. Create a comfortable learning environment by inviting students: *"let me know if you don't understand."* Model and

Remember the 15-30 minute attention spans.

rehearse the behaviors whenever necessary and take note of your vocabulary. You must be sure your students heard what you thought you said and understood what you meant.

Third, make sure your discipline policy is *concise*. Brevity is not only the soul of wit—it's also the essence of good teaching! It is more effective to limit your behavior policy (or any lesson content!) to no more than 3 or 4 'digestible' pieces of information. Keep it simple, and above all, *teach* the behavior, *review* the behavior, and *practice* the behavior. Teaching, reviewing, and practicing behavior is as important with behavior as any other concept you will impress upon your students. Remember that instruction must not only be clear, it must be concise.

Middle schoolers get upset at situations more often than they get upset with you. Always leave the back door open and give them an opportunity to back out of reactive rather than intentional misbehavior.

Fourth, make sure your discipline policy is *consistent*. Middle schoolers thrive on consistency, but consistency may not be something your students are used to. As with desired behaviors, you may also have to model consistency for them.

In consistent discipline, teenagers see not only fairness, but also safety. Consistency in discipline means that you should never take misbehavior personally. Misbehavior isn't usually *about* you, even if it's directed *at* you. Be firm, but flexible, in your discipline. Set a strict standard and don't move the finish line. Also, remember that students act more often from impulse than evil.

Let them think your plans are their idea...this works wonders!

If you are clear, concise and consistent in your behavior expectations, middle schoolers will generally respond positively to whatever discipline policy you employ.

We've discussed student behavior. Now, let's talk about *you*. What can you, as a teacher, do to aid in behavior management?

First of all, become aware of your personal 'trigger points.' Trigger points are those points at which you will no longer tolerate an undesirable behavior. Be sure you recognize such trigger points *before* you become angry. Students will learn the limits of your tolerance as they measure your consistency and will generally stop short of behaviors that trigger consequences. Understand that students seldom desire to make you angry. Middle schoolers seek the comfort that established limits allow, and both you and your students must recognize the boundaries of those limits, which you set in your classroom.

> **LSD works: love, structure, and discipline are cardinal keys to middle school teaching!**

One spring, I took a group of elementary students outside for recreation/reward time and told them they could play anywhere on the playground. I did not clarify boundaries, and I noticed immediately that the children appeared insecure and hesitant to explore. Finally, I decided to establish boundaries for their play and placed large orange traffic cones as arbitrary boundaries that they were not to cross. *"Ok,"* I said, *"you may go anywhere within the orange cones—but you are not go past them."* Immediately, the children spread out within the boundaries and proceeded to enjoy their play. What they had needed was a well-defined limit and a clearly explained expectation. Given these, the children felt secure and became self-directed. Knowing the boundaries of your tolerance and establishing limits for student behavior will streamline whatever behavior management policy you employ.

Second, remember that how you *address* misbehavior will determine much about how the middle schooler *reacts*. Address the child calmly by name. State the misbehavior or infraction specifically, and the school or classroom policy. Finally, state what you are going to do about the misbehavior, and thank the student for compliance. After that, let it go, and return to whatever you were doing. Words *do* count. Sarcasm, name-calling, rhetorical questions and impossible demands only weaken your position.

Third, keep in mind that middle schoolers often react first and think later. Giving students an opportunity to cool off and correct themselves will usually solve more disciplinary problems than writing up every infraction. Give them their *space*—don't get in their face—when they overheat. Always demand respect, however. *Never* compromise on this expectation.

Fourth, decide beforehand how you will handle students without paper and pencils, tardies, talking, gum, restroom breaks, cell phones, lack of homework, etc., and *enforce* your policy. One system to deal with tardies is to keep a tardy book. Students understand they must sign the tardy book when they come in late. A refusal to sign results in a double tardy.[8]

Make sure, however, that your consequences are appropriate, and not excessive. For example, do not write up every student who violates your gum rule, or forgets a pencil! This serves little purpose other than to make your point and overtax your office staff, and will create an adversarial atmosphere in your classroom. Do not attend every battle to which you are invited—you must learn to *choose your battles*. Remember, for the most part—over-correction creates more problems than it solves.

When you discuss your policies and procedures, explain the *why* and *reasoning* behind them. Think like a student in regard to rules—a rule without a reason is ridiculous. You will find students more cooperative if they understand the reasoning behind the rules. In whatever way you choose to handle your policies, be clear in expectation and consistent in enforcement. If possible, utilize reason over power.

Never—*never* argue with students in front of a class or make threats in anger, or that you can't deliver on. Keep private matters just *that!* As soon as you engage in a power struggle with a middle schooler, YOU lose. Trying to lecture, negotiate with, or nag a middle schooler driven by a power struggle will not work. You have the responsibility as the adult to avoid and extinguish power struggles.

Sometimes, the best way to diffuse such a power struggle is to end the conversation and proceed to enforce strict school discipline. Some infractions—such as violation of school rules—cannot be overlooked. Use, however, your authority sparingly and selectively. When you must discipline, make the discipline swift and effective. Also, make sure the punishment fits the infraction. Do not overcorrect, or under discipline. Never threaten, embarrass, berate, or humiliate a student. Always—*always* apologize when you're wrong. Praise *publicly* and admonish *privately*. Discipline the *behavior*; spare the child.

Finally, realize that there will be some students to whom you will not be their favorite teacher. Be realistic. You will not win the battle with every student, no matter hard you try. Nevertheless, clear and consistent discipline will, more than just about anything else, create a positive learning environment in a middle school classroom.

Expectations

Expectations. Set them high. Accept reality.

Years ago, the Western Electric Hawthorne Works in Cicero, Illinois discovered in the business world what teachers already knew. High expectations correlate with high achievement. The *Hawthorne Studies* (or *Hawthorne Experiments*) were conducted from 1927 to 1932, where Harvard Business School professor Elton Mayo examined productivity and work conditions. In essence, the *Hawthorne (or Pygmalion) Effect*[1] can be summarized by stating that student behaviors may be altered by the fact that students know there is a high expectation.

Inspiration + Preparation + Motivation + Expectation = Success!

We all start the year with high expectations for our students, and rightly so. More often than not, your students will rise to meet the expectations you set, so set those expectations high. In the study known as *The Pygmalion Effect,* children aged six to twelve years, all drawn from the same school, were given an IQ test. Children were then assigned to an experimental or control group. When teachers were told that the children in the experimental group were "high achievers", expectations were increased. These children then began to show significant IQ gains over the course of one year, *despite* the allocation to a group having been, in fact, random. In other words, high expectations became self-fulfilling. Remember the lessons of expectation. Students gravitate toward the expectations set for them—whether those expectations are positive or negative! Learning *does* expand to fill expectations—expectations of the teacher—and expectations understood by students.

One year, I had a 5th period class with a large percentage of lower-functioning children. Somehow, the schedule had pooled them into that often 'drowsy' period which meets right after lunch. I decided I would modify—but not lower—my expectations for this class. I would tell the children I expected as much from them as from all my other classes. I raised the bar. At the end of the grading period, not only had this class met my expectations, they had exceeded them. They achieved *despite* limited abilities.

While expectation may not always lead to perfection, it will lead to positive achievement. But also accept reality. Know your students and the limits to their abilities. Do not set unachievable goals that will only frustrate them, but never fail to set genuinely high expectations for your students. Motivate your students to be *better* than they are. If you can make them *want* to be good, your behavior management plan will be easier and much more effective!

Anticipation: Closing the loopholes!

The best cure is still prevention. This axiom is never proved truer than in your classroom. Close all loopholes for misbehavior *before* the misbehavior occurs, and your classroom will function far more efficiently. *Anticipate* the behavior patterns of your students, and you will make the teaching process much easier on yourself.

Seating charts, for example. Seating charts are most effectively used early in the year. They are a better *preventative* of misbehavior than *cure* for unacceptable conduct. You might do better to begin with the traditional *row* arrangement of desks until you learn student names and establish

When you are ready to deviate from the traditional seating arrangement, wide short rows generally work best!

your authority in the classroom. The traditional arrangement *does* limit student interaction, and students placed in the *front* and *center* areas of the classroom tend to ask more questions. I like to seat my students across the *width*, rather than the *length* of the classroom. This creates the shortest distance between me and the back row of students. However you arrange your seating, be cognizant of *traffic patterns*. Middle schoolers gravitate to the path of *most* resistance when going from here to there. Close the

Never—never, leave students unsupervised in the classroom.

loophole. Straighten the path. Eliminate the diversion and reduce your stress. If you establish seating charts early, your students will view them as an aid to taking roll, learning names, organizing cooperative learning activities, and enhancing behavior management. When used as a punishment, however, your class may feel they are *all* being disciplined for the misbehavior of a few. *Anticipate*. Close this loophole.

A second classroom management loophole to close is basic classroom logistics. Be sure your students know early where everything is—the pencil sharpener, Kleenex, assignment board, homework box, etc. Put your clock *behind* your students if possible. Let them know what is off-limits, such as your desk, the stapler, personal belongings, etc. Never assume they know. Teaching your students room logistics early prevents you from having to answer the same questions repeatedly later. (See Appendix A: *How to Survive Opening Day*.)

Middle schoolers love to be read to!

A third loophole in classroom management I learned to close early was reducing the time consumed dealing with missed assignments for students who were absent. Instead of explaining numerous times about the prior day's assignment and what handouts were missed, I posted an 'assignment box' in the back of my room and attached it to the wall. When students return from an absence, they simply pick up the materials missed, which I place in the box. This requires my students to take personal responsibility for this aspect of their education. It also eliminates the opportunity for excuses and frees up my time by closing a loophole.

> It takes a middle schooler three times as long as it would take you to complete a task, and the effective total homework time for middle schoolers is ten minutes *times grade level.* Always make sure homework is authentic, meaningful, begun *in class* and *checked.* Also, posting homework on free websites such as *schoolnotes.com* is a fun and easy way to keep everyone at home abreast of the latest assignments, as well as a way to share interesting web pages!

A fourth classroom management loophole I learned to close was dealing with 'lost' materials left in my room. Instead of having children ask me a dozen times a day if I'd found a lost item, I created a *'Mr. Parks, did you find my...'* box where students always know I will put misplaced items.

A fifth classroom management loophole I closed was in the collection of student assignments. Instead of having to collect and organize papers from my classes, I attached hourly class boxes to my walls. Students put their work in their class box. Time saved. Organization streamlined.

A sixth classroom management loophole I closed was to create a *'new student folder.'* New students generally arrive at your door with little or no notification. To have to restate all your beginning of the year expectations is as impractical as it is impossible. To maximize my time and the new student's transition, I created a folder containing the syllabus for my class, expectations for my classroom, assessment procedures, etc. Again, time saved and organization streamlined.

A seventh classroom management loophole to close is what to do in emergency situations. Do you know how you will handle seizures, bee stings, and the administration of medications? Are you aware of *who* has epilepsy, allergic reactions, or asthma? Have you arranged for your sub to know this information? Remember confidentialities. Know the policies regarding what you can and cannot do in emergencies, and be prepared. Emergencies *will* happen.

> Reward for good behavior. Do not bribe students to 'be good' for a reward.

An eighth classroom management loophole to close is to realize that your students will sometimes have problems you simply cannot—and should not— deal with. In cases of suspected abuse, severe depression, or suicidal tendencies, etc., refer students to the counselor. Never forget that you are a teacher—not a trained psychologist. Don't attempt to solve every problem your students bring to you. Let the professionals deal with the serious ones.

A ninth classroom loophole to close is to eliminate the temptation to meddle! Middle schoolers are extremely curious, and chalk next to the chalkboard, or colorful markers next to the whiteboard, are sometimes impossibly tempting! Keep these out of sight.

A final classroom loophole to close is what I call *'management through proximity'*. This often forgotten and highly effective tool recognizes the importance of you, as the teacher, moving throughout your classroom. Students will behave in a more positive manner when you do not remain stationary. Along these lines, always maintain a 'scan-desk' mentality as you teach. That is, never become so lesson-focused that you don't continually scan the room for problems which may be waiting to happen. Keep your eyes *open* to *close* this loophole. A working 'scan-desk' mentality 'defrags' a multitude of potential difficulties! Management through proximity. Simple, but effective.

Anticipate—close the loopholes. Always keep in mind regarding behavior management when dealing with middle schoolers—an ounce of prevention is *better* than a pound of cure! Anything you can do to avoid difficulties will streamline the process and make your classroom a more pleasant and enjoyable environment for all.

Celebrating achievement: Rewards

While every teacher would like to believe that students learn for the joy of learning, realistically this applies to the very few. Let's face it—the majority of your students would rather be somewhere else besides sitting in your classroom. In dealing with middle schoolers, even the most dynamic teaching personality has its limit and teachers must find other ways to keep students motivated.

While attending an NMSA conference one year, I recall hearing a speaker say, *"Teaching is a selling profession. We are selling a product called education, and the more enticing we make this product to our buyers, the greater will be our successes!"* Whatever may be your personal philosophy on the subject—rewards *do* motivate—especially in middle school! Celebrating achievement builds interest in the classroom, and *interested* students learn more efficiently.

Students are generally motivated in one or more of 6 ways; through: *projects, people, praise, prizes, prestige, and power.*[1] Consider these when motivating and evaluating middle schoolers. Whatever you choose to use, keep in mind that rewards must be age-appropriate. What is positive reinforcement to older teens may not work for younger students. But remember that middle schoolers are still children. Very often, the most effective way to enter a student's mind is through a child's heart—and sometimes, through a child's *stomach!*

I have found that a few small candy bars used as a reward in review-question activities makes this activity not only more effective, but also more enjoyable. Several times a week, I play the *Jeopardy* review game with my middle schoolers. Students try to formulate a correct question for any answer I give them. A candy bar is the reward. I am always amazed at how hard my students will work for chocolate! Not only

> Remember when keeping treats—some students may be diabetic, allergic to certain foods, or have braces. Keep various types of snacks 'just in case.'

does this make learning enjoyable, it is also *performance based.* Performance based learning stimulates higher-level thinking skills. Instead of merely choosing a response (as in the typical review game format) students are forced to generate an inquiry.

While you may feel that rewarding students might tend to reduce intrinsic motivation, this is not the case. *Never forget your audience*—you are dealing with children, and recognition or reward is a wonderful reinforcement tool. Stickers, homework passes, treats, awards, etc., really *will* motivate middle schoolers and are tools you can and should use in your classroom.

Whatever rewards you choose to employ, remember—do not *overuse* them. Rewards should be anticipated, but not assumed. Make sure your students see rewards as reinforcement for positive behavior, not bribes to avoid negative consequences. Overuse of rewards produces ever-diminishing returns. Used sparingly, rewards can bait the hook of learning and motivate your students to achieve. Often the process is as important as the product. Celebrate achievement! It motivates your students!

When all else fails...

Although you control most aspects of management in your classroom, there will be times when such control slips out of your hands. Changes in the schedule, lessons that flop, unexpected weather and fire drills, fights in the hall, your

> Use mnemonic devices. Middle schoolers love these!

unanticipated need for a sub, spontaneous assemblies—all of these will occur when you least expect them. When they do, the best behavior management technique is to abandon your prepared plan and change course. Therefore, always—*always* have a 'plan B'.

Having a 'plan B' will keep things at least on a functioning plane until things return to an even keel. As a new teacher, the last thing you need is to have to devise an alternative lesson in the midst of a crisis or unexpected change in routine. Be proactive—have an emergency or 'anytime' lesson prepared, and make sure whoever is going to need it (including you!) will know where to locate it!

The least I need to know: My to do checklist!

- ❏ I will remember that my students are children first.

- ❏ I will remember that my students will enjoy my class more if they see I truly enjoy what I do!

- ❏ I will never argue with, threaten, or humiliate my students.

- ❏ I will set *clear, concise,* and *consistent* expectations for my students, and state them in a positive manner.

- ❏ I will remember that my students may often not hear exactly what I meant to say!

- ❏ I will strive to create a safe and inviting atmosphere in my classroom where my students are not afraid to ask questions when they do not understand.

- ❏ I will practice flexibility and fairness in my behavior management and give my students the opportunity to correct their own behavior.

- ❏ I will never discipline in haste or anger, and will correct *behaviors* rather than *persons.*

- ❏ I will require my students to respect my *position* as teacher, even if I'm not their *favorite* teacher.

- ❏ I will never compare my students, or play favorites!

- ❏ I will practice *listening* to the opinions and reasoning of my students.

- ❏ I will recognize my own 'trigger points', learn to pick my battles, and to overlook the small stuff.

- ❏ I will always have a *'Plan B'* just in case!

- ❏ I will learn how to apologize to students when I'm wrong and compliment them when they're right.

❑   I will be proactive in closing classroom loopholes before they lead to unacceptable consequences.

❑   I will understand my students' view of rewards, and practice rewards in a timely manner.

3. Support: *Building Parental Resources— help is out there!*

Principle—*"Your most valuable resource is the one you will most seldom use!"*

Lesson I must learn: The parents of your students are an invaluable resource. Utilize and appreciate them at every opportunity, and you will gain the most important ally you will ever have as a teacher!

A short course in dealing with parents

Without question, the most important resources you will have are resources that you seldom see in your classroom. Those resources are the parents of your students. Parents are your students' *first* teachers.

As a newer teacher, you may prefer less contact with parents. Many teachers see parents and parent questions as a challenge to their authority. This, however, is destructive to the parent/teacher relationship. Parents are not opponents, but allies. When parents have questions, let them know their questions are welcomed. Never forget—their concern is for *their* child. Your concern is for them *all*. Recognize that whatever you can do to help parents make *your* job easier will prove to be time well spent.

Always remember to return parents' phone calls and emails, and do so promptly.

The school environment often intimidates parents, but they are the allies you *cannot* afford to be without. Make it a point to invite them to your school. Include them in class activities which involve their children. Provide them with a syllabus of your class and a calendar of school events. Encourage them. They are your most valuable resource. (See Appendix H: *When Conferencing with Parents*.)

I have found it to be helpful in recruiting the assistance of parents, to begin every year with a handout of parent helps entitled 'Chicken Soup for Parenting' (See Appendix I: *First Open House for Parents*.). This mini-instruction manual which deals with homework, Internet resources, study time, etc., gives parents a head start on helping *me* become a more effective teacher of their children.

A second thing I do to involve parents is always to make it a policy to contact them before they need to contact me. Because of the middle school design, teachers tend to have more frequent contact with homeroom parents than parents of students in other classes.

> **Teaching carries with it an unstated expectation that the student has a problem, and the teacher has the solution.**

Nevertheless, I try to send some type of positive correspondence (in addition to progress reports) to parents of every student I teach. This is time-consuming, and sometimes impractical, but the bottom line is—it simply builds good rapport.

For example, to the parents of students who excel academically in my class, or students who seldom receive discipline reports or failing grades, I send home a 'your child is a pleasure to teach letter.' Time and time again, I have been told by parents that they never receive *positive* correspondences from teachers, and that these letters have been copied and sent to grandma, or taped on refrigerators and kitchen bulletin boards. To parents, this simple, positive contact is unexpected evidence that someone appreciates their child. Surprise your students' parents—tell them something *good*. You will gain an ally you cannot afford to be without.

A third thing I do is to surprise parents in a more specific positive way. I will mail home an official school discipline report on a student who exhibits wonderful behavior in my classroom. Instead of describing an offense, however, I will fill in notes of appreciation and praise. The parent is caught by surprise when the 'official' school letter arrives. This action—used sparingly—has proved a positive icebreaker to more parents than I can number.

A fourth thing I do to involve parents is to utilize the parents' careers. Although there will be exceptions, parents generally enjoy coming into my classroom and speaking about what they do for a profession. Don't forget to tell them ahead of time how much time will be available to them, and remember to videotape presentations. Parents may be able to present to only one class. This will enable you to reuse the presentation in other classes, and in future years. *Always* send them a thank you note. Even if parents decline such invitations, you have established an 'open-door' policy, and when a parent feels free to communicate with you, you gain tremendous leverage.

A fifth way to involve parents is to begin each year collecting email addresses. More and more parents are becoming available through email. You will find that being able to contact a parent by email regarding a student's grade or conduct is quite helpful. Parents are far more likely to keep in contact with you through email than by telephone. Email correspondence is also more documentable, and documenting everything is an understood rule in middle school. (See Appendix T: *Important Documents to Keep!*)

A sixth way to involve parents is to invite them to assist you as an aide in your classroom. Allow them to judge exhibitions or projects. Many parents are also quite willing to help with class and school announcements, copying handouts, sorting files, tutoring and monitor students, etc.

A seventh way to involve parents is to send them homework folders which must be signed-off on. These, along with class (not just school) progress reports (See Appendix G: *Parent Alert Notification*), reminder letters, and especially a class syllabus at the beginning of the year, will create a constructive working relationship between school and home.

Finally, consider a school (or team) newsletter. Sending home a monthly newsletter with student-parent challenges, digital photos of students, and timely articles of what is going on at school is a personal and much-appreciated contact.

Empower your students' parents! In allowing them to help you help their children, you recognize them as a valuable ally and build a unique team relationship.

The least I need to know: My to do checklist!

- ❑ I will remember that parents are my most valuable allies, allies I *cannot* afford to be without.

- ❑ I will try to utilize the skills of parents rather than perceive them as the opposition.

- ❑ I will make it a policy to, in some way, contact parents regarding something positive before parents end up needing to contact me.

- ❑ I will send home *thank you notes* whenever they are necessary.

- ❑ I will create at least the atmosphere of an open-door policy toward parents.

- ❑ I will attempt to make my classroom an inviting—not intimidating—place where parents will feel comfortable in coming.

- ❑ I will collect as many email contacts from parents as I am able.

4. Maintenance: *Building Relationships— functioning successfully in the school environment!*

Principle—*"Everything you needed to know to become a teacher—they didn't teach you at the university!"*

Lesson I must learn: 'Big doors often swing on small hinges.' There are small but important things you must remember in order to become a successful teacher, and the way you deal with your staff, duties, and personal responsibilities will determine your success or failure as a teacher. Learn these lessons well!

> ➢ Your two biggest assets within the building
> ➢ And never the twain shall meet
> ➢ The Proactive solution
> ➢ Think before you speak!
> ➢ You'd better take them seriously: *Personal Responsibilities*
> ➢ Substitutes

Your two biggest assets within the building

As a new teacher, you must understand the school environment and personnel that will comprise your home away from home for as long as you teach. The first thing to understand is the distinction between *certified* and *classified* staff. While certified staff (teachers and administrators) may be considered the so-called brains of the school, the classified staff is truly the heart and soul. Get to know your classified staff well. *Appreciate* them even more.

Your most valuable assets among classified staff are—without a doubt—the secretary in the front office and the custodian. Little can be achieved during the course of a school day without them. Make it a practice to do small things to improve their day. Remember to say 'thank you,' and treat them with respect when you enter their domain. Understand that this is their turf, and they don't work for you.

For example, don't wait to do something nice for the secretary (or secretaries) on 'Secretary's Day.' The school will probably do that. Let them know you appreciate them more than once a year. Send them a note of appreciation for no special occasion. Leave them a sweet treat to surprise them, and be sure to bring them a small gift when you attend conferences. Remember how busy they are, and try not to inundate them with requests for things you may be able to do for yourself. Remember to answer the phone in a pleasant manner when you are interrupted in the middle of your perfect lesson—it may be a busy secretary (or a parent!) simply needing information. Return, in a timely manner, such things as your morning attendance list, surveys, locker combinations, purchase orders, and receipts. Failing to do these makes their jobs more difficult. What you may perceive to be mundane or insignificant becomes exponentially more difficult for them when multiplied by the number of teachers involved. Remember, these people keep the school functioning, and they have deadlines too. The effectiveness of their job is not separate from, but often *dependent* on, you doing your part in the process. Learn to appreciate your secretaries. They are your most valuable personnel assets.

Your second most valuable personnel asset is the custodian. Without the custodians, *you* would be fixing what was broken and cleaning up the accidents in the hall. Without the custodians, your room this morning would look the way you left it yesterday afternoon. Practice small acts of courtesy toward your custodians. For example, I always try to straighten my students' desks and pick up much of the stuff kids leave on my floor *before* the custodian comes in. If your room has tables with chairs, be sure the students put the chairs up before they leave if your custodian prefers this. This will make his or her job easier, and you will feel less intrusive the next time you misplace your keys and need your room opened!

Never forget—you have one room to deal with for nine months—your custodians have dozens to deal with year round. They are the experts in building management and take pride in its appearance. Always ask their help when making permanent changes in facets of the building, such as drilling holes for pencil sharpeners, putting nails in walls, etc.

And never the twain shall meet

Your school environment, of course, includes more than merely the secretaries and the custodians. Your school environment is your home away from home. The key here is the word 'away'. A second way you relate to your school environment is how it is affected by what goes on at home. In your school environment, it is vitally important that you remember to never mix concerns at home with responsibilities at school. This is not always easy.

Sometimes that lesson in your 6th period class falls flat, and you think about your poor planning for it all the way home. Sometimes that disagreement with your spouse or children at home follows you to school, and your day starts off on a down note. Sometimes mixing home and school concerns is simply unavoidable, but, whenever possible, try to keep home and school problems separated.

Bringing problems from home to school can affect your teaching. Middle schoolers are especially perceptive and often pick up on things we may not expect. Try to smile often. Smiling does affect your tone of voice and middle schoolers are especially responsive to voice tone. (Very often, the voice of 'Mr. Rogers' can calm the multitude!). It is not possible to always be a bundle of joy when you come into your classroom, but you can at least be cheerful toward your students. Your classroom demeanor and effectiveness as a teacher can be easily affected when things at home affect things at school. Too, you may more readily say something you do not mean, or perhaps lose patience more quickly, when you are tired because problems at home are affecting your job at school. Keep these two domains separated as much as you are able.

In the same way, try not to take your school problems home. You will have difficulty enough with the schoolwork you *must* take home—try not to add problems at school to the load! Your family deserves your full attention as well. Treating school concerns and home concerns as separate emotional environments will go a long way to lengthening your career as a teacher!

The Proactive solution

Another way you relate to your school environment is your attitude towards it and all that environment entails. You will do well to develop a *proactive* attitude. Becoming a proactive teacher in your attitude, actions, and appearance will reap greater rewards for you than just about anything else you can do. You can become a proactive teacher in a number of simple—but highly effective—ways.

> Accept the fact that your energy level *decreases*, and your weight generally *increases*, during your first year. Eat with this in mind!

For example, take the initiative to arrive early to school. It just looks good. Many teachers habitually arrive at school five minutes before homeroom begins. While there may be nothing inherently wrong with this, you will make a positive and lasting impression on your administration and fellow teachers if you make it a point to arrive early. Arriving early also makes you available in case you are needed. Not only can you get more lesson preparation done early in the morning than you would on a busy afternoon, but you'll probably never raise an eyebrow on those days when it becomes necessary for you to leave school early.

A second proactive habit is to invite your administrators (and parents) into your classroom before they come out of necessity. If you create an open-door policy to your classroom, you will feel less intimidated by unannounced visits and visits for purposes of evaluation.

A third proactive habit is to always pay back other teachers with interest. What does this mean? Whenever you borrow items from other teachers, such as paper, paper clips, folders, etc., always return *more* than you borrowed. Pay back 'with interest.' Whenever a teacher covers an obligation or duty for you, don't simply repay the favor—repay it as soon as possible! Payback with interest is a small action that will be remembered.

A fourth proactive habit is to never leave school without at least a start on what tomorrow requires. I am a morning person and plan my day's activities better in the morning than on the afternoon of the day before. But I always strive at least to *begin* the next day's activities before I leave school. This enables me to fine-tune the lesson in my mind before I teach it the next day. Remember, everything you don't put off today becomes unnecessary to do tomorrow!

A fifth proactive habit is to take the initiative to introduce yourself to all personnel in the building without waiting for them to come to you. Know where these people are in your building. The librarians, counselors, coaches, cafeteria workers, the school nurse (if you have one)—all are intricate parts of your professional environment. Get to know them. You will need favors from all of them eventually.

A sixth proactive habit is to volunteer for committees and school duty, rather than waiting to be asked. Such are time-consuming, but they are an intricate part of the teaching duty. They are things you have to do, so look more professional—volunteer! Don't sit and wait to be assigned.

Finally, become proactive in your monitoring of student behavior and activity outside your immediate classroom. Be in the halls between classes. Check restrooms and other areas in your school where students might linger. Don't wait to be asked (or told!). Be proactive. Just do it!

A proactive attitude looks good, accomplishes much, and reaps innumerable benefits. Find as many ways as you can to become *proactive* rather than *reactive*! If you will strive to 'do without having to be asked,' you will reap dividends many times over for the small effort it requires.

Think before you speak

Yet another way you relate to your school environment is through the words that come out of your mouth. Someone has said that our words will get us into trouble long before our actions cause us grief. This is never truer than in a middle school environment. Be very careful what you say around—and about—staff and students. Your words may come back to haunt you.

A middle school is its own micro-community. It is made up of individuals from different backgrounds, different beliefs, and different personalities. What may be funny to one person may be hurtful or even offensive to another. A confidence meant to be kept may damage a reputation if that confidence is betrayed. A rumor spread can create a lasting animosity, and idle conversations may make you enemies.

Always be mindful of *where* you are. Be careful what you say inside—as well as outside—your classroom. As teachers, we become so accustomed to being surrounded we sometimes neglect to see students—or worse, parents—who might overhear a conversation and repeat what we prefer to be kept private. Remember, too, that middle schoolers are children who not only repeat what is heard, but often misunderstand and misquote what they hear.

As a teacher, you are also dealing with an adult staff with which you will be spending many years. Think *carefully* before you speak. Is this conversation inappropriate? Is this conversation unnecessary? Is it something that could be no more than idle gossip? Is this an adult concern that should not be shared with students? Is this something that could be misinterpreted or misconstrued? Reputations—including yours—can be easily damaged by such indiscretions of conversation. If you do have a 'disagreement' with a colleague—air out your differences. Respectfully resolve them as soon as possible. *Never* let them fester! Never pre-judge what you may not fully understand. Listen twice as often as you speak. If there is *any* doubt regarding whether or not you should say something, you will do well to leave it unsaid! It is always easier to defend what you *didn't* say.

Finally, be aware of the attitude you might be conveying to those you work with. Remember, *you* are the new teacher with much to learn. You will be much better accepted by conveying a humble and compliant attitude than by coming off as defensive and pedantic. While you may be fresh out of school, you don't have to act like it!

You'd better take them seriously...

A final way you relate to your school environment is in your performance of duties. As a new teacher, you will learn that teaching is like an iceberg. Dealing with students is merely the tip of a much larger responsibility—the most time-consuming of which involves meetings and conferences. While these may not be as exciting as what you do in the classroom, they are just as much a part of your job description, and you'd better take them seriously.

For example, if you are a part of a middle school team, you may meet with other team members on a regular basis. At times, you might feel as though you could be using your time more efficiently by doing lesson preparation. Nevertheless, you would do well not to opt out of such meetings unless absolutely necessary. When you cannot attend meetings regarding students, at least send information regarding the student's work in your class (See Appendix M: *Student Report Form*). The same holds true for department meetings, detention, bus supervision, Admission and Release Committee (ARC) meetings, school committee meetings, and especially parent-teacher conferences. Some of these duties will require after-school time, but take them seriously and attend. Your peers probably feel the same way you do about them, but for the most part, they will be there, and you should be, too. It looks good, and it's an understood part of your job description.

Faithfulness in the performance of school duties not only *looks* more professional—it *is* more professional.

Substitutes

When you cannot be in your classroom, it is more than simple courtesy to leave your substitute detailed and clear lesson plans (See Appendix U: *Substitute Teacher Form*). It is also the *professional* thing to do. Don't forget to tell them bell schedules, attendance and discipline policies, and whom to seek on your team if they need help. I keep a folder in which I include those documents as well as seating charts, lists of students they can trust, any medical issues that might arise, and lunch procedures. Make sure your students know that when a substitute is teaching in your absence, you are expecting them to be on their best behavior. Let them know their conduct reflects upon you as their teacher.

Substitutes have a difficult job. Do what you can to make their job easier. I also try to also leave a snack or two for subs in my classroom refrigerator.

The least I need to know: My to do checklist!

- ❑ I will make it a practice to show small kindnesses to the secretaries and custodians, and to always treat them with respect.

- ❏ I will make a conscious effort not to mix problems at home with work at school.

- ❏ I will strive to be among the first teachers to arrive at school in the morning and among the last teachers to leave in the afternoon!

- ❏ I will make it a habit to pay back with interest those who lend me things.

- ❏ I will try to get at least a start on tomorrow's lesson before I leave school today!

- ❏ I will be very careful what I say at school, and I will not spread gossip or rumors.

- ❏ I will remember to leave my substitute full and courteous preparation.

- ❏ I will do my best to attend all *504* meetings, Admission and Release Committee meetings, and all parent meetings. I will send my information when I am unable to attend.

5. Content: *Building a Lesson—*
the bricks and mortar
of learning!

Principle—*"An ounce of need will go further than a pound of content!"*

Lesson I must learn: Your familiarity with the subject you teach—and the way you present the information—is the heart and soul of your job. Know your content, and distribute it in a way that is easily digestible to the children you teach!

> ➢ '*Nice* to know or *need* to know?'
> ➢ The Big Picture
> ➢ The *Bloom*-ing miracle
> ➢ The 3 '*R's*'
> ➢ Homework
> ➢ The Socrates Effect
> ➢ Assessment

Nice to know or need to know?

To fail to plan is to plan to fail. It's as simple as this—effective teachers prepare effective lessons.

In preparing effective lessons, your first consideration regarding the information you teach your students is *relevancy*. Are you preparing to teach what you are *supposed* to be teaching? Is this lesson information a part of your subject core content? Is this lesson applicable to the state and national standards in your subject area, or just 'filler material,' e.g., stuff *you* enjoy? Understand that *education*—not mere entertainment—is the job with which you are entrusted and that students do recognize the distinction. While non-curricular information can be interesting as an occasional diversion, never forget—you are being paid, and trusted—to teach the curriculum. *Need to know* always takes precedence over *nice to know*, and you must never allow important information to become victim to the trivial.

Teaching your curriculum presupposes that you *know* your curriculum. It is critical that you become proficient in the curriculum area of the subject you teach. If you know your curriculum, you will be better able to make lesson connections, which are vital to the ability of your students to generalize and apply information. Stay abreast of current research and updates in your area. Volunteer for curriculum committees, test writing, textbook reviews, etc. (See Chapter 1: *Professionalism.*) This will enable you to know and apply your core content, and understand what is expected of you in your classroom.

> Talking with is memorable. Talking to is instructive. Talking at is sedating! If you awaken their interest, and stir their curiosity, you will multiply their learning! Enthusiasm is highly contagious—so also is apathy and boredom. Remember, kids will sometimes find more learning in your light, than in your lesson.

Be <u>very</u> familiar with your state's required teaching for core content in your subject. You should also know the content and concepts for the grade levels before and following yours so that you can connect and lay the foundations for those concepts as well.

Look up and become familiar with the National Standards for your subject. You are expected to do no less as a professional, even if you are not directly held accountable to do so. The increasing emphasis on state testing of students may expose your weaknesses if you do not teach what your students need to know. *You must establish credibility with your students!* Students need to know the core content of the subject area that you teach, and—just as importantly—they need to know that *you* know it.

The Big Picture

Preparing lessons is not an art. It is an acquired skill. It takes practice, but is not difficult. (See Appendix Q: *Sample Lesson Plan.*) One way to make prepared lessons more effective is to utilize 'scope and sequence' in your lesson design. Ask yourself *"what is the overall goal of this lesson?"* In other words, what are the *essential questions* you want the students to be able to answer? Once you have established that within acceptable parameters for the age group you teach, proceed to break down the process by which you will achieve this. Make sure you see the *sum* before you develop the *parts.* (See also Appendix CC: *Presenting the Lesson.*) The scope and sequence also aids your students as well.

> "Teach a lesson, mold a character, shape a destiny."

Tell your students what it is you will be teaching them. Keep them aware of where they've been and where you're taking them. When students know and understand the scope and sequence of a lesson, they are better able to stay focused, set goals, and ask essential questions.

I have found it helpful to both students and parents to provide a syllabus reflecting the units, concepts, and topics to be covered in my class during the year, along with when each unit will be taught. Whether or not your school requires a yearly syllabus, it is still an excellent personal organizer to help you, your students, and their parents understand what you will be teaching.

> **The only application more important to them than present-day application is personal application!**

The Bloom-ing miracle

While we're on the subject of your lesson, consider the simplest—and yet most effective—method you will ever encounter in its creation and delivery. This method was conceived by Aristotle, is universal in its acceptance, and, in truth, comprises the heart and soul of 80% of all the educational research on effective teaching and learning. It's called *Bloom's Taxonomy of Learning* (See Appendix K: *Bloom's Taxonomy*), and it's the finest frame on which you will ever construct a lesson. The taxonomy is hierarchical, that is, it begins in simplicity and advances through complexity. Its foundation goes back to the ancient Greek method of instruction—a method that still works today. Study the hierarchy. Utilize the structure. Plan and construct around its framework and your students will benefit greatly. This taxonomy is probably the finest single paradigm of teaching and learning ever created.

The 3 'R's'

A final element in effective lesson preparation is to understand the audience to whom you will be teaching the lesson.

Middle schoolers have unique mindsets. Their retention spans and interest levels are far different from yours. They generally tend to live in the 'immediate' and have difficulty generalizing concepts and applying lessons as we would like them to. Because such adolescent characteristics often work against that

> **Application is everything! If the lesson isn't applied to their world, it's as relevant as a rock.**

perfectly planned lesson you created, you would do well to remember the *3 'R's'* of teaching a lesson to middle schoolers.

First, your lesson must *relate*. While relating your lesson to prior knowledge, or to another subject in your curriculum is important, your lessons will prove *most* effective when they relate to some thread of relevancy in your students' lives. Middle schoolers relate through *internalizing* information, and internalization is tied to *importance*. As much as *you* might value your lesson, that lesson will generally rate no higher than *sixth* on your students' priority list! The most important priorities in a teenager's life rank something like this: *themselves*, their *friends*, their *family*, their *peers*, and *you*—or the teacher at the moment. The lesson you prepared so carefully is low on their priority list and may rank somewhere down there with *"what time is it?"* or *"when does the bell ring?"* Connect your lesson to that which is important in your students' lives. Remember, if the lesson doesn't relate to something *else* on their priority list, it won't be effective.

One teacher tells the story of how she was waxing eloquent in her most brilliant lesson—captivating (she thought) her audience—holding their attention in the palm of her hand. Suddenly, a student with a surprised look flashing across his face raised his hand to ask the penetrating question, *"Have we had lunch yet?"* Such is the attention span of a middle schooler.

Middle schoolers can only absorb twenty minutes or so of information, and their attention spans are about twice their chronological age, so if you want information remembered, you'd better make that information *relevant!* Something in your lesson must *matter* to them. The best way to relate your lesson is to recognize a channel for their interests and work to fill it!

Research indicates that learning retention rate increases from 35-52% as material is practiced through 3-5 repetitions. We remember 10% of what we hear. We remember 50% of what we hear and see. We remember 90% of what we hear, see, *and* do.

In social studies, for example, the concepts of *change over time* and *historical perspective* are fundamental concepts students must learn. Understanding that the likes, dislikes, and opinions of teenagers also change much over time, I wanted to find a channel through which I could relate the concept. I decided to let them make a *time capsule*. Early in the year, each student filled out a prepared form where they could list popular songs, movies, and events from the beginning of school. I also permitted them to include private things such as romantic interests (certain to change over time!), predictions of grades, and best friends. In a big 'burial' ceremony, the form was then sealed in an envelope and taped into a 'secret' part of their notebook. (I also discovered fewer notebooks were lost during the year!) At some later time, I had the students open their time capsule, and as the students laughed at how *"different things are now!"* the 'change over time' lesson became quite relevant! Why? It related to things important to them. I had recognized a channel for their interests and worked to fill it! The lesson *related.*

The next best way to relate your lesson is to connect it to a current event. For example, during our study of Mesopotamia, we experienced the tragedy of September 11, 2001. Rather than forcing my prepared lesson on confused children, I chose to link the day's events to the history of that troubled area of the world. In doing this, the lesson became far more memorable. *Relate* the lesson and you will impress the learning.

> The first lesson you should learn from your students is to *never assume* they know something! If you're lucky, they'll ask questions! It's better to explain the details again and again, than to build on a foundation that isn't there.

Following these two, the next best way to relate the lesson is to connect it to prior knowledge. Prior knowledge helps the mind categorize information, therefore making it more retainable. Prior knowledge might be nothing more than yesterday's lesson, but it helps middle schoolers see the aim, purpose, and flow of the lesson, rather than appearing to them as mere learning for the sake of learning. However you do it, remember—effective lessons *relate.*

Second, you should never be afraid to *repeat* your lesson. Repeating a lesson does not mean you teach the same lesson over and over. It means that you repeat and rephrase *key concepts* of each lesson in order to make the impression. Your students may complain, but through continual repetition you will hear your lesson in their voices and quickly learn if what they understood was what you *thought* they understood!

> "It is more effective to question their answers than to answer their questions!"

A teacher tells of teaching 6th graders the concept of ancestor worship in the Orient. In reviewing for the test, she made it a point to remind students to review that concept. When students were later asked to discuss the subject in a narrative, many expressed the esteem with which the people in the Orient held their sisters and other female members of their families. The teacher was puzzled by these numerous comments until she realized the children had no concept of the term 'ancestors'! They thought she had been referring to their *'aunts'* and *'sisters'!*

In teaching social studies to middle schoolers, I assumed that my students understood the words to the *Pledge of Allegiance*—something they had repeated each morning for half their lives. I was wrong. While all knew the words, most did not understand the terms 'allegiance' or 'indivisible'. Half their lives. They never knew.

Always practice *wait time* after you question. Research shows that learning is stimulated through the extended pause following a question. As the *wait time* increases, so does student learning!

Never assume that all your students understood what you *thought* they understood. While most may, many will not. If you're *lucky*, they ask questions. Most won't. Remember that *repetition is never redundant*—it's the mother of learning! Very often, it helps you clarify misunderstandings you might never have anticipated.

Another teacher, teaching in a farming community, tells of spending an entire class period teaching 6th graders various phases of agricultural development in another culture. Assuming the lesson to be going well, the teacher asked if there were any questions. Following an excruciatingly long wait, one student raised his hand and asked, *"What is agriculture?"* Redirecting the question, the teacher asked if someone else could explain the term. No one could. Finally surrendering, the teacher gave the class a simple definition of the term. Suddenly, the lights of learning flashed across the faces in her class, and one student replied: *"Well, now it makes sense!"*

Third, make it a habit to continually *review* your lesson, either in bellringers or within the lesson. Middle schoolers love to show what they know—especially when an occasional reward is on the line. I have had success with *Jeopardy* answer and question oral reviews, and always keep a supply of miniature candy bars in my desk to raise the stakes once in a while.

One of the most effective learning devices you can use to stimulate higher level thinking skill is the analogy. For example, have students complete such analogical thinking paradigms as, 'sixty is to six, as a dollar is to what?' Another might be, 'thermometer is to temperature, as (what) is to weight?' or, 'Homer is to (what) as Shakespeare is to *Julius Caesar?*' The use of *metaphor, allegory*, and *comparison/contrast* prompts also show high correlation with student achievement.

One of my favorite review activities is a reciprocal teaching technique I call *'the power of the chalk.'* I challenge willing students to 'teach the board,' upon which I have left the previous day's lesson. I sit in the student's seat, and the student takes my place reviewing the board—chalk in hand. In giving my students the power of the chalk, I learn how effective—or *ineffective*—was the prior lesson. As I sit as a student, I am able to refocus and clarify when necessary. Students love this activity and the 'authority' it gives them! Be prepared, however—this activity will expose every part of your lesson that was not understood or was *unclear* to your students. More than once I have been amazed that what students understood was *not* what I intended to convey! You can never review too often in middle school!

Relate the lesson to build understanding and context. *Repeat* the lesson to transform short-term memory into long-term memory. *Review* the lesson for internalization! These are vital parts of effective lesson planning and teaching.

<u>*Homework*</u>

Before we leave the discussion of teaching the lesson, let's discuss homework. Homework is best defined as *independent, unmonitored* practice. The subject of when to give homework, how much a middle schooler needs, and whether it is even helpful in middle school has been debated in recent years. I have found that ten minutes of homework per grade level per class has worked well for my students. Any more and middle schoolers either become frustrated or balk. Any less and they don't take it seriously. Homework given more than a couple of times per week seems to be ineffectual, but this, of course, is class-specific There is no doubt that repeated emphasis, or *practice* (including homework) on a topic, formula, or concept increases retention rate. Ebbinghaus[9], in an often-cited study years ago, concluded that:

- after 20 minutes—45% of a lesson is lost
- after 60 minutes—55% of a lesson is lost
- after 24 hours—70% of a lesson is lost

Ebbinghaus used his own experiences as a source of data. Nevertheless, his approach to self-study was carefully controlled. However you decide to assign homework, remember that:

✓ Homework should be started in class.
✓ Homework should never be *punishment* or *discipline.*
✓ Homework should *count*, but be added—never subtracted—from
    a total. Students should always be able to keep what they've earned.
✓ Homework should be discussed and accounted for the next day.
✓ Homework should count for no more than 15-30% of the grade.

The Socrates Effect

Your lesson is only as good as the impact it makes on student learning. Do not see your lesson as mere information to be converted into a teaching 'bullet' and fired at your students! This is *not* teaching. Teaching involves more than delivery of information. Teaching involves creating a new perspective in the thoughts and minds of your students.

Socrates was a famous Greek philosopher. He was also an effective teacher. Socrates taught—not just through delivery of information—but also through stimulation of *inquisitiveness*. Instead of filling a vacuum with information, he *created* a vacuum of challenge into which the natural inquisitiveness of his students plunged! In a teaching technique that bears his name today, Socrates forced his students to come to their own conclusions by means of skilled questioning methods—the *Socratic Method*.

> Grades do not always fully reflect either good teaching or learning well. Grades are only as good as the assessment system that formulates them, and should *never* be a tool of behavior modification. Sometimes, keeping the score is not always as important as cheering the process!

Learn how to question your students in ways which will enable them to *reason, analyze,* and *apply* information. Challenge their minds by making them *explain*, not just answer. (See Appendix BB: *Summation of Standards: the WOW Classroom.*) For example, in my social studies class, I try to ask more *why* than *what* questions. I ask students to paraphrase or rephrase—not just repeat—information and concepts learned in class. When a student asks a question, try asking another student to *rephrase* that question. In doing so, you not only generate thinking, you also check for understanding. Later, as your students come to conclusions, inquire as to possible *effects* and *alternatives* of their conclusions. Ask them to *defend* statements they make in class by citing *examples*. Instead of merely feeding information to your students, try challenging them with questions which force them to *analyze* and *explain*. You will be pleased with the increased retention rate!

Assessment

Student assessment is a necessary and important part of teaching. It can, however, sometimes be intimidating for students and can create a 'you against us' attitude between students and teacher. This attitude, you need to change as early in the year as possible. Be sure you go over your assessment procedures with your students early in the year, and review them often. Post your grading scale. It is also important to make sure assessments are not perceived something negative. Testing is to find out if students have accomplished objectives of an assignment. If your students learn to not perceive assessment as something negative and intimidating, you will create a more relaxed assessment atmosphere, and students who are relaxed assess more efficiently.

APPLY, APPLY, and APPLY! "An ounce of need is better than a pound of content!"

Early in my teaching career, I noticed that students almost always perceived test-taking as a negative experience. I wanted to change this perception, but how could I make the dreaded test-taking process enjoyable?

First, I had to consider my audience. I was dealing with middle school children, where, more often than not, the more off-the-wall the activity, the more enjoyable they find it!

Second, I needed to choose an aspect of test taking to employ my activity. I knew middle schoolers often hurt scores on quizzes by misnumbering answers, or failing to include their name. In an effort to eliminate these occurrences, I created my 'grinch trap.' I tied a string to the ceiling and attached a clothespin, a pencil, and a giant paperclip. As they marveled at this conglomeration hanging over their heads before our first test, I told my students about the grinches, which lived in our ceiling! These grinches, I explained, were hairy purple creatures that dropped into students' ears on quiz days, and caused them to make careless mistakes on assessments—even when they knew the material. Before every quiz, I would now set this trap, and the trap would now prevent them from being 'grinched'! The students stared at me in silent disbelief. Throughout the assessment, I could see them trying *not* to look up at that grinch trap. When the assessment concluded, I wondered if this off-the-wall effort would serve its purpose for my students—to make assessment more enjoyable, and to reduce careless mistakes. My effort accomplished its purpose so well, 'setting the trap' has become a ritual in my class, and I dare not give an exam without performing it!

Another way to avoid the 'depressing assessing' attitude is to practice assessment that is *authentic*.[10] Authentic assessment has a real-world *purpose* and relates to the goals listed in your lesson (See Appendix N: *Ideas for Spicing Up Instruction*). Authentic assessment does not test simply to be testing. Assessment must be (and be recognized by your students as) more than a mere regurgitation of facts. It must stimulate higher level thinking skills whenever possible and challenge your students to excel.[11]

For example, do not always give just quizzes. Some students are more performance-oriented. Allow them to create a model, work up a PowerPoint presentation, demonstrate a concept, present orally, conduct an interview, make a video, develop a webpage, or research the Internet. Internet scavenger hunts are always a hit. Modify to your class content. When you must test in the traditional manner, vary these methods as well. Multiple choice, true false, short essay, fill in the blank, and open response questions may be alternated or combined. For example, I discovered that giving open-note quizzes on occasion proved quite revealing. Not only did it reinforce the importance of note-taking and keeping up with and bringing notebooks, it also added the element of surprise and established self-confidence in many of the lower-achieving students. Why? They recognized that fulfilling basic classroom instructions paid off for them *academically.* Varying assessments not only eliminates the boredom of routine, it also addresses the multiple learning styles of your students.

Never let a 'teachable moment' pass without milking it for all it's worth!

Generally speaking, the retention rate of middle schoolers decreases as assessment paradigms are utilized in the following order: *personalized information, analytical thinking information, hands-on activities, conceptual material, factual material, and irrelevant (in their eyes) material.* Assessment material that <u>relates</u> is the finest assessment of all. Assessment does not have to be depressing in middle school. However you assess, remember too—students who are relaxed assess more effectively.

It is also important to help your students understand that assessment isn't just about evaluating them—it also helps you evaluate what *you* are doing to help *them.* Let your students know that assessment helps you become a better teacher. When middle schoolers understand that assessment helps everyone, it becomes less intimidating. Always make sure your students see and understand the rubric by which they will be graded.

Second, however you choose to assess, it is important to provide your students feedback *immediately* and *often.* Students will learn more effectively when feedback is provided as near to the lesson learned as possible, and when they see it as a regular routine. It is especially effective in middle school to personalize feedback comments as often as you are able. Though time-consuming, there is powerful influence in a *personalized, positive* comment on a middle schooler's paper! I have found this to be much more effective than mere grading alone. When you personalize with a note or a comment, you are planting seeds which will result in the harvest of a positive relationship in the future. Make sure to return graded papers to students as soon as possible. Delayed feedback results in diminished effectiveness.

Finally, make your students understand that passing is the responsibility they must take. Provide every opportunity for your students to succeed. Address multiple intelligences and extol improvement, but resist the temptation to give what is not earned. Your students will learn neither responsibility nor the content through academic welfare.

The least I need to know: My to do checklist!

- ❏ I will remember in teaching my subject the difference between *nice to know* and *need to know*.

- ❏ I will be familiar with my subject core content, as well as state and national standards in my subject area.

- ❏ I will stay abreast of the latest research in my area.

- ❏ I will remember that scope and sequencing is a very effective organizational technique—both for me and for helping my students to learn.

- ❏ I will never forget that, in middle school, *relating* the material is the fundamental prerequisite for learning.

- ❏ I will remember that in teaching middle schoolers, *repetition* is never redundant.

- ❏ I will remember that if I don't *check* homework often, it will evolve into *no* home 'work' at all!

- ❏ I will understand that if my students don't understand—if I'm *lucky*—they'll ask.

- ❏ I will never forget that an ounce of need goes further than a pound of content.

- ❏ I will remember the more enjoyable the review is, the more effective will be the retention.

- ❏ I will practice asking my students more questions rather than merely feeding them information.

- ❏ I will practice *authentic* assessment, and vary my assessment techniques.

☐ I will remember that *review* of material can take on many forms.

☐ I will never forget that middle schoolers vary not only in their learning styles, but also in the way they respond to differing assessment models.

☐ I will post my grading scale, and go over assessment procedures with my students *early*—and *often*!

☐ I will remember in assessment to praise *progress*, and understand that a little encouragement goes a long way.

6. Attitudes: *Building Atmosphere— creating a magical environment!*

Principle—*"As a teacher, your job is not to fill a bucket, but to light a fire!"*

Lesson I must learn: Your attitude toward your subject and your students is the most important key to student achievement. Your students will often learn more from the fire of your presentation than from the information in your lesson. Be excited! Enjoy what you do!

> ➤ Attitude Creates Atmosphere
> ➤ The P.I.E. of Successful Teaching
> ➤ Inviting Room or Grant's Tomb?
> ➤ Descending the ivory tower

Attitude Creates Atmosphere

The most important thing you will create in your classroom is not your perfect lesson plan, your reward system, or your wall décor. The most important thing you will create is the atmosphere of a learning environment where you and your students will spend the next nine months. Like it or not, your classroom will become a micro-family, with you as one parent and learning as the other. Classroom atmosphere will determine whether the learning experience is positive,

Color, Creativity, and Caring will take you further in middle school than just about anything else. Remember these '3 C's'. Kids *love* the first, *enjoy* the second, and *need* the third!

negative, or exists at all. The micro-family which is your classroom may well be a more inviting environment that many of your students' families at home. Be an inclusive teacher—toward *all* your students—not just the ones that are popular or make good grades. Make each one feel they have a purpose in your 'family'—let them play a part—even if they simply want to erase a board, or straighten your rows. The atmosphere your students perceive when they walk into your classroom will affect them, and the way they learn, the rest of the year.

One way to create a positive atmosphere is to establish an *active* learning environment. The most negative learning environment you can create is to do nothing more than assign a task, threaten a test, discipline by the seat of your mood swing, and work at your desk until you are forced to get up and flick the light switch. A good teacher *engages* students, *establishes* behavior management, and *encourages* success!

Another way to create a positive classroom environment is to encourage your students to be respectful enough to use 'thank you' and 'please' in their conversations. Remember though, if you want it—*model* it! Such courtesies not only foster positive personal habits, they also just make everyone *feel* more special!

> Keep 'high walls,' 'small doors,' and 'wide yards' toward the students. Be sure they know you are in authority, but give them space to be creative and express themselves. Allow them a small but vital 'open spot' into discovering you, the teacher, as a real person. Never be afraid to try something new, silly, or 'on the spot.' The more they see what you're trying to do, the more respect you will earn. It's still true: they don't *care* how much you *know* until they *know* how much you care!

A third way to create a positive atmosphere is to understand that a silent classroom doesn't always indicate a positive classroom environment. Sometimes it indicates diligent learning. At other times, it indicates fear.

The *Pax Romana* was the 'peace of Rome.' It was a famous period known worldwide as a time of unparalleled splendor among the Emperors, and peace among the inhabitants. But the peace was an uneasy peace. Most parts of the empire did not challenge Rome due to fear, not due to satisfaction.

Mr. Steele was my science teacher in 7th grade. His classroom was so quiet visitors often thought he was on planning period. None of us dared talk without permission. This is nearly all I remember about Mr. Steele's class. This is not to say he was a poor teacher, or that quiet classrooms are not effective learning environments. But I never felt comfortable in an environment where I was silent out of fear.

> Fifty years from now it won't matter how rich you were or what car you drove. What will matter is that the world will be a better place because you were important in the life of a child.

Before you assume that silence is always golden in a middle school classroom, be sure you understand that sometimes an active classroom is a classroom where students feel secure enough to discuss, while a quiet classroom sometimes indicates they are too afraid to care. Some students learn best through speaking, not merely listening. They are external thinkers whose voiced expression works for them as a personal review technique.

Attitude creates atmosphere. How you deal with diverse situations goes a long way in creating atmosphere in your classroom. Foster an attitude of *flexibility*. Understand that, by its very nature, middle school is a world of flux and change. Your perfect lesson plan will be interrupted. The student who most needs to stay in your room will be called to the office. The phone will ring in the middle of your best lesson. Also, foster an attitude *of patience*. Never overestimate how quickly your students learn, or underestimate how much even the most academically challenged students can grasp.

Finally, foster a *sense of humor*. Don't take yourself too seriously. Relax a bit. If you blow it once and awhile, don't be afraid to laugh at yourself. Be silly in front of your students once and awhile. They will love to see this in you. Sometimes a sense of humor can save the day for you—and your students.

The P.I.E. of Successful Teaching

Good teachers know how to combine three other ingredients to create a successful teaching atmosphere in a middle school classroom. Note that I didn't say a *survivable* atmosphere in a middle school classroom—you may survive without these— but these ingredients create a successful atmosphere. I call this my *'P. I. E. of successful teaching'*.

> The *P* stands for *perseverance*.
> The *I* stands for *inspiration*.
> The *E* stands for *enthusiasm*.

Perseverance is the most important personal attitude you will develop as a teaching skill. Perseverance alone is what will get you through those inevitable times when your good lesson meets a bad day, and the

"Success is very often 20% aptitude and 80% attitude."

whole thing flops. Try to remember that such days happen to all teachers, and that to simply persevere is often your only alternative. On other days, you will arrive late, inadvertently insult the secretary, embarrass the custodian, let a perfectly good teachable moment slip away, slip and fall on a wet spot where you mopped up vomit, forget your department meeting, and have the assistant principal spend two periods in your classroom observing your students forget everything they learned yesterday! Remember too, that such days will always be balanced by days when the lesson you least expect will make an impression—succeeds! Never let discouragement build a nest in your self-confidence as a teacher. Push on through those days when you wonder if perhaps you should have gone into another profession. Hang in there! The most valuable lessons you never planned to teach your students might well be the patience, courage, and endurance you show under fire. Though you may not feel like it, smile, compliment, encourage. On those days when nothing seems to go right, remember—no matter how little you feel you have influenced a child's life—you *have* made an impression. *Persevere!*

> A spoonful of sugar *still* helps the medicine go down! Whether reviewing or testing, if you can *make it fun*, students will be more productive...it's the nature of the 'beast'!

Inspiration is the second piece of the pie of successful teaching. It is the most important attribute you can foster in your classroom! Let me say it one more time—inspiration is the most important attribute you can foster in your classroom. Remember, you will teach more effectively through *inspiration* than through *perspiration*. Middle schoolers are inspired by things they *enjoy*, things by which they are *challenged*, and adults who elicit *respect*. You will inspire your students to excel in each of these three ways.

> The element of *surprise* is one of the most important things you can utilize in a middle school classroom! Keeping them on their toes is fascinating, exciting, and effective! *Routine* is the substance of a middle-schooler's life. They thrive on *consistency*, and consistency makes the occasional *diversion* that much more exciting!

Enthusiasm is the final slice of the pie. Enthusiasm is contagious. So is boredom.

I remember when I was in middle school, a few of my teachers seemed to have suffered from a 'charisma bypass'! They taught in 3-D: *dry, dull, and disjointed!* Not every teacher can have a magical personality. Every teacher can, however, inject some energy, courage to be creative, and enthusiasm into their lessons. Just as a yawn is picked up by others, so also are joy and excitement. Try teaching in a different type of 3-D: *dynamic* (put some enthusiasm into the lesson), *digestible* (break concepts down into smaller tidbits), and *developmentally appropriate* (remember, middle schoolers are still children).

Middle schoolers are uniquely sensitive to the tiny, often imperceptible cues we give them every day. A nod, a raised eyebrow, and a frown—all these convey a message. Students pick up on and are affected by most of these cues without ever realizing it! Likewise, genuine enthusiasm becomes contagious in a middle school classroom. Students can become excited about learning whether they consciously choose to or not!

Your middle schoolers will come to you with some measure of enthusiasm. Much of what they bring will be due to individual personality. Unfortunately, much of what they've *lost* will be due to the classroom attitudes of their former teachers. In becoming a good teacher, learn how to build on what each student brings to you. Become enthusiastic about the job you do and the lessons you teach! As you do, you will watch your students become more receptive learners. *Channel* their enthusiasm, don't dam the flow! Relate to their interests! Remember, your students are people too. Never sacrifice the child for the sake of the student.

> Balance creativity with organization in your classroom. Don't be so creative that you're not organized, or so organized you're not creative.

The *'P. I. E. of successful teaching.'* Perseverance, inspiration, and enthusiasm. Three vital ingredients for creating a successful teaching atmosphere in a middle school classroom, and instilling within your students the joy of learning!

Inviting Room or Grant's Tomb?

Walk into your classroom, and pretend you are seeing it for the first time though the eyes of a thirteen-year-old. What feeling does your room convey? What emotions does it evoke? Is your classroom clean, inviting, colorful, and (reasonably) organized? Or is it drab, dull, and more like a tomb than a room a middle schooler would enjoy spending 7% of his or her life in?

Your students will enjoy learning far more in a colorfully decorated classroom, and anything you can do to help students enjoy the learning process will be a large bonus in your favor! Take the time to decorate your room. Make it middle school friendly! (I have two locker mirrors on my file cabinet—one marked 'boys', one marked 'girls'!) Put up some pictures and a colorful bulletin board. Put your name outside your door. Next to my door I have a small sign that reads, *"Through these doors pass the most important people in the world—my students!"* Also be aware of the lighting and *temperature* of your room. Small things such as these create an inviting atmosphere for young teens and get things off to a positive start *before* your students even walk through your door!

Also, display significant honors that you may earn. You are your students' teacher—they want to be proud of you! Your diploma was only the beginning. Let everyone who walks into your room know that you are proud of your profession and your accomplishments. Displaying your honors will not appear to your students as vanity on your part. It will give them a sense of pride that they've had a part in your success and in making you what you've become!

Descending the ivory tower

Yes, you are a professional—never forget that. But you are also a teacher of middle schoolers—older *children*—never forget that either. Come down from the ivory tower of educational solemnity every once and awhile. Play with your students. Don't be so academically minded you become no classroom good!

> *Examples* are foundations in learning's temple, and *illustrations* are windows to the sanctuary!
> "The average teacher TELLS. The good teacher EXPLAINS. The great teacher DEMONSTRATES. The master teacher INSPIRES!"
> (W. Ward)

Remember, those seats in your classroom are filled first by *children* who happen to be your students. They are children *first*, students second, and children need to be able to relax at times within a structured environment. Recognize when it's time to relax. Don't kill their hearts by pounding their heads. Tell a story or two from when you were young. Post a photo of *your* school days. Create a magazine cover of you and your students. Never be afraid to laugh at yourself when the occasion warrants. Illustrate a point with a personal reference, and never forget that illustrations are windows to the mind—even for adults—*especially* for children. Some of my most effective lessons were illustrated by failures in my own life. Open up a little. Always remember—*you* are more important than what you *teach*, and some students will be motivated by the hero you have become in their eyes. Model effectively. Be a professional, but let the kids peak inside a bit.

The least I need to know: My to do checklist!

- ❑ I will do my best to make my students look forward to coming into my classroom and be glad they're here.

❑   I will remember that, in the middle school classroom, *attitude* creates *atmosphere*, and that I have the ability to create or destroy an effective learning environment.

❑   I will understand that a quiet classroom may not indicate a successful learning environment, and that an active environment may not be indicative of ineffective behavior management.

❑   I will make my classroom an inviting place to enter.

❑   I will encourage *courtesy* in my classroom—and practice it myself.

❑   I will strive to be flexible, patient, and to cultivate a sense of humor.

❑   I will endeavor to inspire my students to achieve, and never forget that my job is not to fill a bucket, but to light a fire!

❑   I will seek to enjoy what I do each day, and understand that enthusiasm is especially contagious in the middle school classroom.

❑   I will allow my students to get to know *me* a bit.

7. Strategies: *Building Learning—strategies that make it work!*

Principle—*"Learning should be enjoyable! Make sure you don't kill their heart by pounding their head!"*

Lesson I must learn: There is no perfect way to teach a lesson. It is the diversity in teaching strategies that make every classroom unique. However, a few strategies have stood the test of time, and are universally helpful in making students enjoy—not merely endure—the learning experience. Utilize and modify what has worked in the past to create new and innovative ways to teach your subject!

- ➢ *Numero Uno* on their list!
- ➢ Empowering your students—the fuel that runs their engines!
- ➢ The *'5-10-15-20'* rule!
- ➢ Teachable Moments
- ➢ Lay down a challenge
- ➢ Cooperative Learning
- ➢ Shock their socks off!
- ➢ *'Dead Poets'* DO speak!

Numero Uno on their list!

What is the most important thing to middle schoolers? Is it their friends? Is it their clothes? Is it their reputations? Believe it or not, none of these is the most important thing. The most important thing to a teenager is their *name*, and the second most important thing is the work of their hands. Learn their names—their *preferred* names, and pronounce them correctly. This may seem a simple and non-vital function, but it is a powerful motivator. Keep a bulletin board to post student work or achievements. Be sure you have a place for student photos, which they will give you, and a place to display especially touching notes of appreciation. These show students you care about them as individuals, and not merely as collection of students whom you must teach.

> In the spring, the 'sap' rises and the energy level drains in middle schoolers. *Keep them busy!*

Empowering your students—the fuel that runs their engines!

Teenagers are often the very definition of chaos! They are random motion, jumbled emotions, predictable unpredictability, and organized confusion. They often seem to run on hormones and gum, and their engines sometimes seem to never run out of gas. But the most effective fuel that runs a middle schooler's engine is not sugar, free time, or hormones, however.

The fuel that runs their engine is the fuel that you as a teacher can give them with no fear of calorie counting, parent complaints, or lawsuits. The fuel that truly empowers a teenager is *encouragement* and *praise*. Encouragement should be unconditional, and can make a middle schooler feel significant when they are frustrated, or feel they've failed. Praise is conditional, and based upon success. It fosters the middle schooler's dependence on the opinion of others. Ninety-five percent of the individuals your students encounter on a school day will *not* offer them an encouraging word. Their fuel tank will run on low most of

> An ounce of *positive feedback* is worth more than a pound of criticism. Unfortunately, it won't be remembered nearly as long.

each day. Help fill their tank with encouragement. Encourage your students to be the very best they can be. Encourage them to do better on the next quiz, or during the next grading period. Be especially encouraging when a reticent student raises his or her hand to ask a question. Remember, they are taking a chance that the question might appear silly to their peers! Find something to praise in *every* question asked—even if it's just in the asking of it. Middle schoolers are highly impressionable when it comes to encouragement and discouragement. Foster the first. Eliminate the second.

The '5-10-15-20' rule!

Middle school is an environment where very young teenagers must sit for six or more hours in a structured environment, refocus at least that many times, and endure teachers of varying teaching abilities who love their subject infinitely more than the student does! Young teenagers are also social creatures, and are quick to accept

> Mood swings are rapid in middle schoolers!

compromises when they recognize they stand to gain. In practicing time management, remember the first. Channel the second. Life will be easier for everyone in your classroom.

One of my most successful time-management techniques is one you might find controversial. I call it the *'5-10-15-20'* technique, which may be modified to suit any classroom. My students know that the first *five minutes* of class are theirs. They may socialize as long as I have no problem with volume. To keep this privilege, however, they understand that the next forty-five minutes are mine. Within that time block, *ten minutes* is for review time, where I assess prior knowledge through a questioning game, or 'oral quiz.' This is *feedback time* for me. The next *fifteen minutes* are for introducing new material, such as handouts or board work. Students learn the agenda (and the *purpose* for the agenda—*why* is always important in teaching middle schoolers), which I always post on an agenda board. I then set expectations by verbalizing expected outcomes, such as *"by the end of class...".* This time is also used for review and re-focus, based upon previously learned material.

> **What you say during the *first* and *last* few minutes of a given class period will be what students are most likely to remember.**

The final *twenty minutes* is reserved for any combination of the following: discussion time, application and review of new material, small group or independent work, assigning and *practicing* tonight's homework. This is followed by *closure*. Closure is your final summary of the completed lesson highlights. It impacts *retention* and makes *connections* to objectives.

The *'5-10-15-20'* technique allows students time to be social, but what is more important, it lets them know I understand their needs. It also shows them I care enough to allow them part ownership in our class time, but expect concerted, on-task diligence in return. Through a mere five minutes of compromise, I create an atmosphere of improved learning.

The *'5-10-15-20'* technique also allows direct teaching time to be more inline with the attention-span of middle schoolers (generally twice their chronological age), and restricts *information overload*. Information overload is a detrimental—not just ineffective—teaching habit. It reduces comprehension, and is one of the biggest mistakes a new teacher can make. Information overload is the attempt to cover too much *information* in too short a *time.* When you find your students are starting lose focus, you need to change course. You can always finish the lesson tomorrow. Remember, your goal is to teach your *students* the information—not just to teach the *information* to your students. Your job is to not merely to 'feed a head', but to *enrich a life!* Brevity is the key to dealing with middle schoolers. Maximize your point, and move on.

However you establish your time management policy, be sure you establish it as a classroom *routine*! Establish early—and remind often—your policies regarding pencil sharpening, copying assignments, bringing materials, etc. Middle schoolers thrive on procedure and consistency. Establish a channel of routine in your classroom, and the students will fill it.

Teachable Moments

The atmosphere you create in your classroom goes a long way in enhancing the learning environment for your students. The way you plan your lesson, the consistency with which you handle behavior, interruptions, etc., creates an atmosphere of safety and security. In such an atmosphere, middle schoolers thrive. There will be times,

Always save the fun stuff for *last*. Even the most dynamic personality can't compete with a puzzle!

however, when the learning environment is improved—not reduced—by a spur-of-the-moment *change* on your part. That moment when a lesson plan is sacrificed for a more productive moment for learning. That occasion when fate unites an unexpected occasion with a hunger to know among your students, and an out-of-the-blue opportunity becomes more valuable than your finest lesson plan. Recognize these times when they occur, for they are a teacher's best friends. These are *teachable moments*, and they must be utilized to the fullest.

My lesson was on the concept of democracy in ancient Greece. This was one of my favorite lessons, and I assumed the students would feel the same. I waxed eloquent on the privileges of free speech, rights of the individual, and the importance of the individual voice in the democratic process. My whole class was bored to tears, and many were put to sleep by my profound knowledge. I saw one of my best lessons sinking like the Titanic, when a thirteen-year-old suggested: *"How about letting us debate one of these?"* Not in the lesson plan, but that middle schooler brought to my attention the value of *'the teachable moment'*—that moment when the finest lesson plan must be amended in order to capture the lesson in a way which one moment in time dictates.

Recognize genuine teachable moments. Do not confuse them with those 'divergent paths' that middle schoolers are so expert in leading teachers down. Teachable moments are rare and wonderful expeditions along a more creative road to learning. To utilize them, a good teacher cannot be afraid to sacrifice routine upon the altar of opportunity.

Lay Down a Challenge

It is said that you can lead a horse to water but you can't make him drink. That analogy is sometimes applied to middle schoolers—we make them come to class but say we can't make them learn. Wrong. Put a bit of salt in the horse's water and he'll drink and drink—why? Because he *wants* to. Create a thirst to learn something in a middle schooler and watch what happens! How do you do this? The 'salt' that will inevitably make a middle schooler thirsty is the creation of a challenge. Middle schoolers are experts in finding a point to disagree with. One of their favorite words is *'why?'* With high-strung middle schoolers, as with a river, it is generally easier to redirect the current than to dam the flow. Channel their innate inquisitiveness—do not stifle their creativity. Challenge them occasionally to disagree with a statement, and defend their position. State something as a rule and middle schoolers will find an exception. Stimulate their thinking! Follow the path of middle schoolers' innate curiosity! Play the devil's advocate to create controversy. Force them to think at a higher level.

For example, in our philosophy unit, I had students defend (agree or disagree with) the statement: 'God cannot make a rock so big that even He can't move it.' Students immediately took sides and debated this philosophical dilemma. I followed up the activity with challenging open-response questions using *'why?'*, *'predict,'* and *'what if?'* prompts. Middle schoolers love a challenge. Use this to your teaching advantage.

Cooperative learning

Cooperative learning is a useful and effective strategy for learning. It is a part of what is called *constructivism*, or self-directed learning. It is a learning strategy that is *not* easy to master. While cooperative learning has its place when effectively and sparingly used, too often it becomes an easy way to hope students are learning, when, in actuality, a teacher has not spent the time necessary to prepare a lesson.

> Never sacrifice the teaching of fundamental information on the altar of cooperative learning. Hands-on is very important, but what they enjoy must not substitute for what they need. They may learn from each other, but *you* are the teacher!

Use cooperative learning *appropriately* when you use it. Limit your groups to three to five students. Make sure students understand there is a common task requiring interdependence, and that each role will be assessed. (Roles might include:

illustrator, checker, reader, reporter, timekeeper, recorder, encourager, etc.) Teach the process, and provide written instructions with clear rules and directions. Provide adequate materials, establish a time frame and stick to it. Be sure to assign specific tasks in order to ensure involvement. Finally, require a product—make sure students know there was a purpose—and have them report group findings to the class. Cooperative learning only functions effectively when there are *expectations, procedures, responsibilities,* and *accountability.* Whenever you use this strategy, reserve time for whole-class discussion afterward.

Shock their socks off!

Interested in a strategy that will really make an impression on your students? Want to tell them some things they *never* thought they'd hear? Try this. When you make a mistake—any mistake—say to your students *"I'm sorry."* And when they ask you something about which you don't have a clue, say: *"I just don't know."* Middle schoolers think their teachers either know it all, or *think* they know it all. To admit you made a mistake, or that you don't know every answer, will not only endear you to your students, it will also teach them it's OK to sometimes not be perfect. They shouldn't expect you to be, and you won't expect it of them. Don't over do this, but humble yourself a few times in front of the class, and your students will think *more* of you—not less.

'Dead Poets' DO speak!

Here's an activity that will pay lasting dividends in your classroom and allow you to relax without students while you learn it! It involves *teacher* homework, but you'll be a better teacher for the effort. Rent or purchase a copy of the 1987 Peter Weir film *Dead Poets Society*, starring Robin Williams. It's the story of an English teacher who doesn't quite fit into the conservative prep school where he teaches, but whose charisma and love of poetry inspire several boys. Even if you've seen the film, watch it again. Really watch it. As you do, write down every characteristic Williams exhibits which you feel makes him a memorable teacher. See how many of these strategies *you* might be able to adopt in your classroom. I have listed the characteristics (See Appendix AA: *Characteristics of Teaching Excellence*),

> An ounce of *'why'* stimulates more learning that a pound of *'what'.* However, *'why'* is an unrecognized guest if *'what'* doesn't answer the door.

but it would serve you well to find these on your own before you peek. A second excellent film, though not quite as instructive, is *School Of Life* (2005).

Never forget, teachers who are remembered are teachers who leave a positive impression about learning, and isn't this why you entered this profession in the first place?

The least I need to know: My to do checklist!

- ❑ I will never put strict lesson planning ahead of teachable moments, and I will learn to recognize teachable moments whenever they come.

- ❑ I will remember that while cooperative learning has its place, and is often an effective learning experience for middle schoolers, how I set it up, assign roles, and assess the process is of paramount importance to its success.

- ❑ I will remember that I am the teacher and am paid to be the expert in my subject area and classroom.

- ❑ I will remember that to my students the most important thing is their name, and I will seek to learn each quickly.

- ❑ I will cultivate encouragement in all my dealings with my students, for it is the fuel that runs their engines.

- ❑ I will challenge my students through higher level thinking skills.

- ❑ I will understand that middle schoolers are social creatures, and that allowing my students a bit of free time within a structured environment can create very effective leverage in encouraging them to use *my* time wisely.

- ❑ I will remember that in teaching middle schoolers, it's easier for my lesson to run long, but *better* for it to go short!

- ❑ I will learn to apologize to my students when necessary, and to never be afraid to admit it when I just don't know an answer.

- ❑ I will 'dare to be different' from the average teacher, and learn from others I see to be good at what they do.

8. Teaming: *Building Unity—*
the sum is greater
than its parts!

Principle—*"The broader the foundation, the taller the construction!"*

Lesson I must learn: Working with other teachers in a team setting can greatly improve not only your effectiveness as a teacher, but also the ability of your students to broaden their learning experience. Use the leverage of interdisciplinary teaming to make your students multidimensional learners!

> ➤ Fitting In, and Firing Up
> ➤ Together—we *can*!
> ➤ Collaboration

Fitting In, and Firing Up

If you are fortunate enough to be a part of a teaming environment, you have an opportunity to multiply your effectiveness in teaching your middle schoolers. Teaming offers many benefits to you, but such benefits will require adjustments on your part. As a new teacher, you will face certain expectations in becoming a team player. Remember, fitting in with other team members is only the first step. Your main challenge in teaming is to fire up your students in a way that would not be possible in a non-teaming environment.

Some students will actually learn without notes...if you're good! Research has shown, however, that *note taking and summarizing* are two of the most powerful skills students can cultivate, and the more practice—the better.

As the newest member of a middle school teaching team, your primary role is to fit *their* team. If you ever hope to elicit change, your team must see you as an integral part of the group—not as an intrusive faultfinder. This team has been a home to them, and you are coming in as the new roommate. To become a team player, help your team identify a common vision. Ask yourself where it is you want your team to go, and what it is you want your team to accomplish.

The primary benefit of teaming is to help all team members learn the cognitive and affective strengths and weaknesses of your students. Groupings of students take on differing personalities and styles, and students perform differently in different environments, to be sure.

One year, our team had particular difficulty in dealing with a new group of 6th graders. Many team discussions took place regarding how we would manage them. Finally, the science teacher, while assigning projects, stumbled upon the answer to our dilemma. We had been attempting to control behavior by shutting it down. Through the projects created by the students, however, the science teacher discovered this group of students learned best through *expression* rather than restriction. We had been dealing with the students in exactly the

> **Remember—more often than not—middle schoolers really don't like themselves. They are quite sensitive, and even casual teasing can be hurtful.**

wrong way. Because of the lack of control we perceived in other areas in which we dealt with the students, we had been afraid to encourage expression through activity. The science teacher, seeing the students in her environment, solved the dilemma for the entire team. Such is the strength of a teaming environment.

A second benefit of teaming is the teaching and reinforcement of social behavior. As a teacher, your job is not merely to teach your *subject* to your students. Your job is to teach your *students* your subject, and, what is more important, how they might become well-rounded contributors to our society. Teaming allows you to share with—and learn from—experienced teachers on handling and shaping behaviors as your students move though diverse settings.

A third benefit of teaming is the ability to employ consistency in team policies, which may, or may not, differ from regular school policies. These policies might include how your team decides to deal with discipline, homework, field trips, newsletters, parent meetings, social activities, and block scheduling. Remember, consistency is king in the middle school environment.

A fourth benefit of teaming is the ability to employ cross-curricular instruction. Middle schoolers learn more efficiently when similar material is taught in different classes. The ability to present differing aspects of common themes greatly enhances diversity in student development and adds a multi-dimensional flavor to what it is we want middle schoolers to learn. This allows students to *generalize* and *apply* information.

A fifth benefit of teaming is the recognition that every child has a different personality, temperament, and disposition. Teaming allows students to relate to particular teachers with similar personalities, or experiences, and learn to accept other teachers whose personalities they may not so easily relate to. In this way, students learn to deal more effectively with the real-world environment they will face.

Teaming is more than merely division of responsibility—it is multiplication of opportunity! It is the pooling of expert knowledge across a middle school curriculum, and provides for your students a unity within a diverse atmosphere, which *is* a middle school.

Together—we can!

If you are part of a team, you are part of a sharing environment. Your input becomes an integral part of the group personality. As part of a team, your contribution shapes the decision-making process, and the sum is free to become greater than the individual parts.

Successful student learning takes place to the extent by which teachers *plan* together, *discipline* in consistency and unity, and *problem-solve* together. *Planning* is the key. *Goals* are the essence. *Flexibility* is the requirement.

Without a shared vision, strife may divide team members, and goals may not be realized. Teams function best as a symphonic unit, whose instruments must be played in harmony. Important questions for successful teaming include:

- What are we trying to teach?
- How are we going to achieve our goals?
- How will we recognize if we are being successful?
- What role does each member play in the process?
- How will we evaluate success?
- Is each subject area represented in the endeavor?
- Is it *necessary* for each subject area to participate?
- How about a team newsletter?

If your students perceive you and your colleagues as a team, and the unit as important, they will buy into the process.

Collaboration

Before we leave the subject of teaming, never forget—the teachers who collaborate with you are a part of your team also. Never leave them out when considering schedule changes, field trips, team activities, etc.

Never forget that your collaborative teacher answers to Federal guidelines and has an obligation to students which is sometimes quite dissimilar to yours. Make sure you keep and follow your IEPs. You—not just your collaborator—are responsible for them.

A sample letter of shared responsibilities that I give to my collaborating teachers is included in the Appendix. (See Appendix V: *Sample Collaborative Teacher Information Letter*.)

The least I need to know: My to do checklist!

- ❑ I will remember that I am a part of a team, and that my input is a valuable contribution to the group, as well as to student learning.

- ❑ I will remember that I need to fit in with the team, and value the contributions of the other members as much as I would want my input to be valued.

- ❑ I will remember that compromise is necessary to teaming successfully.

- ❑ I will remember that no matter what I do, I won't be able to please everyone I work with.

- ❑ I will be sensitive to the importance of my teammates' personal planning time.

- ❑ I will keep a team-meeting notebook, and not assume I will always remember important dates, activities and information.

- ❑ I will be careful not to reprimand a student under the supervision of another member of my team.

- ❑ I will not make teaching difficult for my teammates by constantly making kids late for their classes.

- ❑ I will be tolerant of personality differences and personal teaching philosophies of my team members.

- ❑ I will show up at team meetings!

- ❑ I will remember not to criticize or gossip about the people I have to work with on a daily basis.

❏ I will never forget how much work my team leader is saving me, and I will surprise them with little goodies once and awhile.

❏ I will not isolate myself from my teammates by constantly working on other things at team meetings.

❏ I will volunteer for team duties without always having to be asked.

❏ I will always remember to share the credit—and the responsibilities.

❏ I will remember to acknowledge my teammates' birthdays, successes, and personal recognitions.

❏ I will recognize, support, and respect my collaborating teachers as an integral and important part of my team.

❏ I will take IEPs seriously.

9. Diversity: *Building Background Recognition— not every student brings an identical package*

Principle—*"A teacher can never understand what motivates a student at school until he/she understands the 'hidden rules' of the economic class in which that student was raised at home."*

Lesson I must learn: The economic diversity of the students in your classroom is based upon patterns of unspoken clues and habits extant at home. Understanding these patterns and teaching expectations will enable your students to become more successful academically, as well as socially, in the middle school environment.

> ➢ What Ruby Payne's Framework is *not*
> ➢ Motivational and driving forces of your students
> ➢ Managing behaviors
> ➢ Successful strategies

What Ruby Payne's Framework is not

A Framework for Understanding Poverty by Ruby Payne[12] revolutionized how teachers were able to recognize student diversity. It was not a book on racial or cultural diversity (although cultural diversity is implied), but on understanding the background regarding the economic 'packages' students bring from home into the classroom.

Payne's premise is that economic class is not a continuous line, and not clear-cut in distinction. Rather, it is comprised of what she calls 'generational' and 'situational' poverty schemes. She sees 'poverty' as the extent to which one does without resources, and is quick to note that the paradigm against which such resource availability is measured is relative.

Generational poverty is the entrenched social condition in which the student is merely the next generation of economic poverty stemming from a line of inherited family conditions. *Situational poverty,* on the other hand, is a current (perhaps temporary) condition of economic poverty from which the student and his/her family may or may not transfer. Students from a background of generational poverty are a more difficult challenge. While Payne bases her research on patterns, she is quick to point out that all patterns have exceptions.

Understanding this, Payne identifies certain 'hidden rules' of economic class which our students bring to school. She feels understanding these will help the teacher to better comprehend just why some students are unmotivated, unorganized, inattentive, undernourished, speak inappropriately, etc. In theory, if these 'hidden rules' are understood, students can be taught accepted rules of behavior. This will enable them to become more successful at school and work.

Motivational and driving forces of your students

According to Payne, the 'hidden rules' of economic class which students bring with them to school are the unspoken cues and habits of their 'group'. Economic groups are identified as: *poverty, middle class*, and *wealth.* The differing values and perspectives placed on various aspects of life not only influence how students and their parents behave, but also give some insight into how they think.

The motivation and driving force of each particular economic group may be summarized in the following chart:

	Poverty	Middle Class	Wealth
Driving Force	Survival, relationships, entertainment	Work, achievement, financial security	Social connections, financial gain, politics
Language	Casual; about survival	Formal; about negotiation	Formal; about networking
Possessions	People (Money is to be spent)	Things (Money is to be managed)	Unique items (Money is to be invested)
Time	Now (Decisions are to be made based on survival)	Tomorrow (Decisions are to be made based on future ramifications)	Tradition & Heritage (Decisions are to be made partly based on tradition and decorum)
Personality	Human emotion	Achievement	Personal connections
Family Structure	More matriarchal	Generally patriarchal	Finance takes precedent
Education	Valued, but abstract—not reality	Crucial for climbing the ladder of success & making money	Necessary for tradition & maintaining connections

Managing behaviors

Although it is beyond the scope of this book, listed are some (sample) important suggestions for managing behavior in children from backgrounds of generational poverty. Remember:

- ❏ Discipline is seen as more to elicit penance and forgiveness—not necessarily behavior change.

- ❏ Many behaviors stem from survival outside of school, and the importance of self-governance is diminished.

- ❏ Stress what is simply unacceptable, and suggest alternatives.

❑ Teach that behavior involves choices, and choices involve consequences.

❑ Utilize color-coding, checklists, and reflection activities.

❑ Teach students to use 'adult voice' of resolution and options, not accusation, insult, and attack.

Successful strategies

Here are some strategies which you may choose to employ in considering Ruby Payne's model. How you choose to utilize them will be up to you. You may want to consult your team members as well as your collaborating teacher for ideas.

Successful strategies for working with families from generational poverty might include:

➤ Offering more structure and individual choice
➤ Evaluating resources available
➤ Gathering background data from more than one source/individual
➤ Teaching coping strategies, and providing time-outs
➤ Respecting the student's loyalty to friends, and family (which may not be present in the student's daily life)
➤ Assisting in developing support teams
➤ More use of stories, metaphors, and illustrations
➤ Utilizing team interventions
➤ Avoiding direct questioning
➤ Avoiding power struggles
➤ Providing mentors
➤ Using adult (authoritative) voice

The least I need to know: My to do checklist!

❑ I will remember to treat *all* my students equally and fairly in a consistent manner.

❑ I will remember that my students bring diverse economic packages into my class, which may affect how they view learning, and how they learn.

- ❏ I will remember that different driving forces motivate my students.

- ❏ I will remember that because of differing backgrounds, some of my students may not interpret or understand a question in the same framework as I asked it.

- ❏ I will remember that these differing driving forces affect the parents of my students, and how those parents might view me, my subject area, my discipline procedures, and my school.

- ❏ I will remember that 'poverty' is complex in its definition and varied in its application.

- ❏ I will remember that there are exceptions to every rule, and will treat each child as an individual, not just a part of a 'group'.

10. Real Professional Development—
tips from the top!

Principle—*"It is better to learn from the mistakes and the wisdom of others than to learn from your own mistakes over time."*

Lesson I must learn: Picking the brain of numerous successful teachers with decades of middle school experience can save you infinite time and heartache. Here are lessons from experience—as well as general tips—to make your first year a more successful year!

$$\frac{\text{Respect}}{\text{Time}} = \text{confidence} \rightarrow \text{excellence}$$

As the old adage goes—there's no point in reinventing the wheel. It is much easier to learn from the experiences of other teachers than to go through many of the same mistakes yourself.

While I have included numerous personal tips throughout this book, the following have been solicited and collected from numerous sources. Many are from my teaching colleagues. Some are from teachers I have met and worked with at national conferences over the years, and others are found in the books for new teachers listed in the bibliography. Few of these tips will be new to experienced teachers.

Not every teacher will agree with every tip, thought, recommendation, or comment. Too, some are geared to individual teaching styles, subject areas, and unique teaching situations. Some tips overlap, and none are guaranteed to work 100% of the time. Nevertheless, they are offered to be tried, tested, and refined by *you*—the new teacher.

"What I wish the experts had told me my first year of teaching...."

❑ Never assign a permanent seating chart till after Labor Day.

❑ Place your four most difficult kids in seats at the four corners of your room. Seat best friends in the same row with a seat in between.

❑ Middle schoolers will remember the first and last thing you say, so make it memorable.

❑ Teaching from the back of the classroom once in a while is a good attention-getter.

❑ Special needs students should be placed as closely as possible to where the teacher most often *stands.*

❑ Admit it when you don't know. Your students will have already noticed that.

❑ Try leaning forward as you are acknowledging a student's response to your inquiry (active listening). Students will subconsciously interpret this as sincere interest.

❑ Never make important decisions when you're tired, stressed out, or on Friday afternoons.

❑ Try using a photo seating chart for your sub. Saves many problems.

❑ Middle schoolers will remember everything you say in a whisper.

❑ Use your authority sparingly.

❑ Don't hit a fly with a bat. Discipline appropriately.

❑ In cooperative learning, have students regularly report on progress or they will simply 'shoot the breeze.'

- ❑ Role-play is a powerful teaching tool.

- ❑ Do *not* assume middle schoolers know how to read an analogue clock!

- ❑ Avoid focusing on the smartest kids in your class.

- ❑ Utilize nicknames for students. It's what we do when we care. Address them as such in the halls. Middle schoolers love any personal identification. Just make sure it's positive.

- ❑ Invite a parent to lunch. Works wonders.

- ❑ You tend to call on kids in rows down the middle and across the front. Keep that in mind with seating charts.

- ❑ Develop, the first week, non-verbal cues such as gestures or signals which your students learn to recognize immediately.

- ❑ Strive to eliminate boredom, apathy, and frustration, and you will solve 90% of your discipline problems.

- ❑ Don't use tests as threats. This is non-productive over the long haul.

- ❑ Never assume middle schoolers know how to take a multiple-choice test.

- ❑ One of the best ways to pique student interest is to omit punch lines, leave a comment incomplete, and utilize the phrase: *"I'd better not say... "*.

- ❑ Always keep an extra pen or pencil in your mailbox, and a hidden stash of copy paper in your classroom. You'll be surprised how often these will come in handy.

- ❑ Sitting at your desk raises your behavior problems and reduces your approachability in the eyes of your students.

- ❑ Never underestimate the power of silence or the effectiveness of the *teacher's stare!*

- Never punish the whole class for the misbehavior of a few.

- Keep a question box in your room for kids to write what they will not ask.

- 'Move and monitor' is one of the simplest, most underused but highly effective behavior management techniques a teacher can practice.

- Selective hearing will reduce your frustrations and lengthen your career.

- Color-code whatever you can.

- Pace one side of the room as you ask a question to the other. Great focusing technique.

- Never assume the quiet student is a compliant student, or that they are understanding the lesson.

- Understand that you will purchase the majority of your own supplies.

- Develop 'linebacker eyes'. Survey the situation beforehand, and don't get so involved in what you're *doing* that you miss what is *happening.*

- Have an understanding with your team as to what belongs to team members, and what belongs to individual teachers only.

- Dress for class as if you were going somewhere important!

- Never teach a lesson in isolation. Link it and they'll think it.

- Discipline with a merciful hand first. Never cut a rope that can be untied.

- Take the road less traveled. If you want to be remembered, think how the average teacher would teach a lesson, and then teach it differently.

- At the beginning of each new year, tell your students how honored you are to be their teacher.

- Never allow students to call you by your first name. Familiarity does breed contempt.

- Every lesson teaches *something*—even if the learner is you.

- Always solicit an opposing opinion during student discussion.

- Remember birthdays. This goes a long way.

- When addressing a class speak toward the center of the room. When conferencing with an individual student, always come down to eye-level.

- Treat individual issues through individualized attention. Don't sacrifice the herd by chasing the stray.

- Pause often during a lecture and ask students to write about the topic. Then, ask for responses from those who have not contributed comments.

- Never argue with a student in front of students. What you gain from the one will be lost on the many.

- Yes, stickers *do* work with middle schoolers; duh!

- Make politeness a high priority in the classroom. Use (and require) 'please' and 'thank you' to be spoken regularly.

- If you want it—*teach it!* (Students seldom rise to meet expectations they don't know exist.)

- Compliment with hidden flattery. For example: *"anyone as smart as you should…"*, or *"because you always seem to understand…"*

- Don't give up on a student because of poor academic performance. You have no idea the lessons you might be teaching, or the differences upon a life you might be making.

- Use students to teach a class—especially as a review.

- Use *'us'* and *'we'* more; *'I'* and *'you'* less.

- Simplification and pacing are two words you'd do well to write as reminders on the cover of your planning book. They are too-soon forgotten in dealing with middle schoolers.

- Never make a threat you cannot legitimately carry out. Bluffing eventually *always* gets called.

- Collect as many emails from parents as possible early in the year.

- Remember, a kind word or a hug from you might be the only encouragement a kid will get all day.

- Inserting a touch of humor into a test will break the tension and increase the focus.

- Be quick to apologize—slow to accuse.

- Never seat middle schoolers where they have visual access to grass, sky, or other middle schoolers.

- Impress them with your genuine love for teaching, not your degrees or accolades. It's still true—they don't care how much you know till they know how much you care.

- Know your stuff. Kids can spot a fake a mile away.

- Never underestimate the effect of a positive note home. You'd be surprised how many times these end up on the fridge!

- Never keep your room unlocked or your kids unsupervised.

- After your best lesson, work on how you can make it better. Never presume.

- Never hold a grudge. Every day is a fresh new start to a middle schooler.

- ❑ Always have a 'sponge activity' to soak up extra time.

- ❑ Control the thermostat to make your classroom a learning environment—not an instrument for complaints.

- ❑ Never forget that sometimes the best gift you can give a kid is hope.

- ❑ Have a 'new student' folder ready with rules, a syllabus, textbook info, initial assignments, etc., and what you wanted other students to understand on opening day.

- ❑ Keep a monthly homework assignment board where every kid can see it.

- ❑ Never be alone with child in your room—especially with the door closed. If you need to speak privately with a student, have an adult witness.

- ❑ Keep things simple! Complexity is the enemy of comprehension.

- ❑ Try making a 'video sub' lesson. Teach them when you're absent!

- ❑ Motivate middle schoolers? Create a little competition.

- ❑ Pacing is one of the most undervalued skills of good middle school teachers. Change deliver pace every 10-15 minutes.

- ❑ Leave all your biases at the door. You'll be amazed, in ten years, how surprising some of your students turn out!

- ❑ Utilize free technology - *Google* docs, maps, calendar; etc. Also www.office.live for *Microsoft Office* online or *Open Office* for free compatible files with *Microsoft Office* documents.

- ❑ Consider using student contracts with performance goals clearly stated.

- ❑ Establish grading systems and grading scales early, and note them often.

- Discover your own style as a teacher. Imitation is *death.*

- During lectures, pause to have students tell other students what you have presented. Remember—middle schoolers *do* learn by talking—not just listening.

- Don't give an 'A' if the work is not a worthy and meritorious goal each student should strive for.

- If you want it to be effective—if you want it to be remembered—touch an emotion.

- Follow the IEP. Follow the IEP. Follow the IEP.

- Changes in weather, and the phases of the moon, affect middle schoolers. Believe it—or not—but it's true.

- It's OK to be a little eccentric, a little weird. Stand on your desk; decorate your ceiling; dress up for emphasis. The average teacher leaves little impression. Have the courage to be memorable.

- Use humor, but never at the expense of a student.

- Moderate your praise. Too much creates immunity.

- It's easy to go long in a lesson, but better to go short. The lion that tries to catch two rabbits gets neither.

- Teach and model organization! Explain how to be successful in your class, and reward it.

- To a middle schooler, a comment on a paper is worth as much as the grade.

- Don't assume middle schoolers know how to study—95% of them don't!

- Try ending class five minutes early. It's generally non-productive time anyway, and it can add years to your career.

- Use a couple of the giant 'dollar store' pens as your 'I don't have anything to write with' solution. Kids won't walk off with them.

- Do not waste your students' time. What they 'appreciate' in the short-term, they will resent in the long.

- Never celebrate the highs too much or let the lows bring you too far down. Always steer at an even keel.

- Keep your lessons 'stirred'. Dividing them up with an occasional break will multiply their effect.

- Even if you can't be happy on a given day—be cheerful. It's contagious.

- Keep *Ziploc* bags of various sizes for a multitude of purposes. These can hold a lost tooth, a broken necklace, organize field trip items, keep game pieces from getting lost, etc.

- Never talk about another teacher's class in a negative way—it will always come back to haunt you.

- Remember, middle schoolers will reflect your mood, passion for learning, and relaxation level in your classroom!

- Never underestimate how potent *anticipation* and *suspense* are as motivators to middle schoolers.

- Never leave chalk in the tray, or white board markers within easy reach of middle schoolers.

- Middle schoolers can digest about three pieces of new information effectively at one time. Pause, discuss, review and restate before moving on.

- Utilize exit passes, phone a friend, punting, etc., when calling on kids. If a student tries and misses the question, and another student gets it right, go back to the first student and have them clarify or restate it.

- ❑ Strive for excellence—not perfection.

- ❑ Never discuss a student or their grades through emails to other teachers. If you must—use initials.

- ❑ Use *tinkle tickets* for emergencies only.

- ❑ Develop a basic list of 30-50 vital vocabulary words vital for students to learn in your subject area. Post them, use them, them review them, assess them and drive them home!

- ❑ Require your students to keep their own grades in a notebook or organizer.

- ❑ Begin each class with a review, and cite the purpose for new lessons.

- ❑ Utilize acronyms (and be creative). Kids will laugh at them—and never forget them either.

- ❑ Remember, the kid you find hardest to love is probably the kid who needs it most.

- ❑ Respect takes many years. Don't rush it. Build it.

- ❑ Never change a child's impression of you by a hurtful word or an inappropriate remark. Be careful. What you earn over a lifetime can be lost in seconds.

- ❑ Review, restate, and summarize completed lessons at the end of class.

- ❑ Some kids will work just because they like you. Be thankful.

- ❑ Recognize the difference between sticking by your guns, and being just plain stubborn.

- ❑ At the end of summer, post a supply list inside a school window for what students are going to need.

- ❑ Always return student work *promptly,* and *personalized.*

- Keep your planning books, and include anecdotal notes and stories that worked—and didn't work. These will become a goldmine for your future lessons.

- Never forget—repetition is the mother of learning! Never forget—repetition is the mother of learning!

- Find a way to establish (early) a positive bond with difficult children. Such will serve you well in possible future dealings with their parents.

- Never miss an opportunity for a *sincere* compliment.

- Dare to be creative. More students have died of boredom than from teacher error.

- Better to staple than to paperclip.

- Remember, to a teenager, *everything* is a crisis. Don't belittle their issues. Sometimes it's good to examine a situation through the perspective of young teenager.

- Don't sweat the small stuff. Jammed copiers, *"Please excuse this interruption..."*, homeroom forms and handouts. Remember your real job.

- Remember to refill the paper you use in the copy machine.

- Never underestimate the efficacy of surprise when teaching middle schoolers!

- It is generally more cost-effective to purchase multiple *inexpensive* staplers and one *quality* pencil sharpener.

- Keep crayons as borrow pencils. The kids hate them.

- Send discipline referral forms home—and to the principal—for positive behavior. Kids and parents love these.

- Never let the important become victim to the trivial.

- ❏ Three things you'll always forget: empty the sharpener, refill the stapler, and where is the remote?

- ❏ Always keep a telephone log of parent phone calls.

- ❏ Find something to praise in every question they ask, even if it's just in the asking it.

- ❏ Your classroom is a family: you are one parent, the lesson is the other.

- ❏ Establish your lunchtime routine early and be consistent. If you don't, this can be your most difficult hour. Kids are gearing up as you are wearing down.

- ❏ If the copy machine breaks while you're using it, and you don't know how to clear the jam, make sure you tell someone before you leave it. This is common courtesy.

- ❏ The most powerful teaching asset you will ever own is your reputation – but that takes years. Be patient. Build it.

- ❏ Be prepared to improvise on a moment's notice.

- ❏ Be careful what you say in class. Speak as if you were being recorded. With today's cell phones—you might be.

- ❏ Turn your back as little as possible.

- ❏ Posting kids' work is a potent motivator.

- ❏ Do locker cleanouts in homeroom once a month or so. You'll be surprised what missing things show up.

- ❏ Develop the courage to use 'wait-time' for reflection and comprehension.

- ❏ Create a 'dark side' persona only to be used when nothing else works. Show them the dark side *only* when necessary—but *when* necessary. Even if they never see it, kids need to know it's there.

- Remember the short attention span of middle schoolers (generally twice their age). Teach half as much, twice as well.

- Laugh at yourself. Students don't mind seeing you in a bit of difficulty if you don't take yourself too seriously.

- If you think being a teacher is easy, you probably aren't a very good one.

- The first lesson the kids ever taught me in middle school was to never assume—*anything!*

- The world's two best inventions for teachers—the electric pencil sharpener and the *Scantron* machine!

- If possible, put your clock in the back of the room.

- Never raise your voice, lower your expectations or avoid dealing with a serious behavior violation.

- Make them smile. A happy teenager is more willing to learn. Joy draws kids like a magnet, and most classes are *endured*—not looked forward to.

- Write personal notes of specific praise and encouragement. Even when kids forget your lesson, they will remember this. So will their parents.

- Try to bait every lesson with a hook: a story, question, startling strategy, surprise, quiz, visual, analogy, illustration, challenge, prop, or use of some type of media.

- Be loyal to the district that's paying you. This is ethical if nothing else.

- Never touch an angry kid, or step between two irate middle school girls.

- Specificity *('eyes on me'; 'please stop tapping your pencil')* is always more effective than generalities *('could I have your attention, please', 'please be quiet')*.

- ❑ Make them think it was their idea!

- ❑ Establish close relationships with other new teachers, and find a mentor.

- ❑ Preview any and all media you show to middle schoolers!

- ❑ Always begin tomorrow's homework in class today.

- ❑ Make sure your students understand the impact a zero has on their grades. Middle schoolers don't understand that one zero and two perfect grades still results in a failing score.

- ❑ Keep growing as a teacher. Teachers are like temperature—either rising or declining.

Teachers & kids are people too—final thoughts

Your room is prepared. Your energy—piqued. That first lesson of the year is begging to be taught, and you are excited about having a wonderful year!

Though you will make more than your share of mistakes this first year, with experience, you will undoubtedly become an excellent teacher. Just remember—such excellence does not come quickly, and the road to reaching it is often paved with rough spots along the way. Learn to distinguish between the things you can change and learn from, and the things over which you have no control.

One thing over which you may have little or no control is how other teachers respond to you. Of course, you should do everything you can to earn the respect of your colleagues *(Chapter 4)*. This means you will sometimes need to apologize when you are wrong, and practice a little humility when you are right. But just as you will unavoidably have personality conflicts with certain students you teach, so also you will find that not all your colleagues will warm up to you as you might hope. Teachers are people too, remember, and personality conflicts are just a fact of life in every profession.

Don't be discouraged when some colleagues find fault with you when you've done your best, or when another teacher is not as skilled in apologies as you are. Don't take it personally when another teacher seems to enjoy disagreeing with you at every opportunity. Remember, your job is first to shape the lives of young people, and that should be the thing that concerns you most. Let go of the things you can't control, and be the best teacher you can be.

Finally—never forget—you are there to teach your students *first*, and your subject, second. While core content and assessment are the essence of what you are being paid to teach, they are not *all* you teach.

You are in the life-shaping profession, and, as a middle school teacher, your influence is especially vital. While even your best lessons may not be remembered in a year, *you* will be. And not just for one year, but for the rest of your students' lives. You will not be everyone's teacher of the year your first year. However, you will plant seeds of admiration and respect in your students, which—like fine wine—will season over time, and become your most treasured of memories someday. Your students will remember how you shaped their lives by your influence—and the person you were—longer than they will remember the information you fed them.

Be the best teacher you can be. Just remember that teaching shapes a life—it doesn't just fill a brain. You are a *teacher* – not just a textbook wired for sound! Always remember that.

Appendices:
Handouts and Supplementary helps

Here are some sample forms, handouts, checklists, and letters that have been collected and utilized over many years of teaching. Some may or may not be useful to your teaching assignment, and many you would think of on your own if you had the time. A few lists are compilations from other sources which I have endeavored to site. Selected ones are personal pieces of information I give to my middle schoolers which you may or may not find helpful. The information in some of this material is intended to make you a better teacher, and middle schoolers better students. Other information is simply to help you make more effective use of your time.

Appendix A

How to Survive Opening Day

- ❑ Did I set my alarm clock and watch to the school bell schedule?

- ❑ I will arrive to school early to be very sure I'm ready.

- ❑ I will remember to smile!

- ❑ Do I understand that 70% of the impression I make will be made on this first day?

- ❑ Do I know my first day's schedule for lunch, classes, dismissal and absentee reporting?

- ❑ Does my room appear colorful, challenging, and inviting through the eyes of a thirteen-year-old who must spend a year of his/her life in it?

- ❑ Do I have my name written on the board?

- ❑ Do I have enough desks?

- ❑ Do I have extra pencils and paper for students who may not have them?

- ❑ Do I have my room rules condensed down to the top five and have them posted?

- ❑ Do I have my temporary class roster, and have I gone over name pronunciation?

- ❑ Do I know my table assignments in the cafeteria for lunch?

- ❑ Do I know my lunch time?

- ❑ Do I have individual class schedules ready for each student?

- ❑ Do I know what to do with students who don't have a schedule?

- ❑ Am I aware of any health concerns or medication requirements my students may have?

- ❑ Am I fully cognizant of my district and school rules, policies, and procedures?

- ❑ Do I have a temporary seating chart?

❑ Do I have (or want) an icebreaker activity?

❑ Do I have a plan for homeroom forms, locker assignments, etc?

❑ Do I have a lesson plan for day one?

❑ Do I have an emergency lesson for a sub or myself?

❑ Do I have an inviting sign outside my door with my name, subject and grade?

❑ Do I have an adequate supply of board markers and erasers?

❑ Do I have a plan book, calendar/organizer, and grade book?

❑ Do I have a plan for monies collected?

❑ Do I know what to do about lunch money?

❑ Do I have a posted emergency escape plan for fire and severe weather?

❑ Do I have a list of important phone numbers that I can find quickly?

❑ Do I know what to do in case of a discipline problem?

❑ Do I have the room temperature at a comfortable setting for 25 to 30 excited teenagers?

❑ Am I prepared for *Murphy's Law?*

Appendix B

Things I Need to Make Sure My Students Know on the First Day:

❑ First day gum, bathroom, and tardy policies

❑ A list of supplies I want students to bring to class daily

❑ Back to school activity

❑ Cafeteria expectation policy for my lunch group

❑ The agenda board —what to expect and what to do with that information

❑ Expectations/Routines for class behavior (their behavior, dismissal, pencil sharpening, etc.)

❑ What they should do with/about backpacks

❑ How students are to treat the physical plant of my room (desks, books, trash, etc.)

❑ Location of necessary items— *Kleenex,* pencil sharpener, wastebasket, lost & found

❑ Dress code

❑ Policies: Grading, nameless papers, dismissal/bells/locker times

❑ Hands off items

❑ Missed homework policies (homework buddies, materials, etc.)

❑ Phone use rules, how and when to call home

❑ Notebook organization

❑ Electronics within my classroom

❑ My pet peeves

❑ Syllabus for this class

❑ Use of *schoolnotes.com* or other websites / homework hotline numbers

Appendix C

'Here they come' opening day supply list

- ☐ All-purpose cleaner
- ☐ Calculator
- ☐ Can of air freshener
- ☐ Chalk/white board markers/erasers
- ☐ Color pencils
- ☐ Construction paper
- ☐ Correction fluid
- ☐ Desk calendar
- ☐ Dictionary
- ☐ Double-sided tape
- ☐ Erasers
- ☐ Extension cord
- ☐ First aid kit
- ☐ Glue
- ☐ Highlighter
- ☐ Hole punch
- ☐ Masking tape
- ☐ Note cards
- ☐ Paper
- ☐ Paper clips
- ☐ Paper towels
- ☐ Pencils and Pencil sharpener
- ☐ *Plasti-Tak* (several packs)
- ☐ Room locker mirror
- ☐ Safety pins
- ☐ Schedule for the day
- ☐ Scissors
- ☐ *Sharpies*
- ☐ Small pack of 'Thank You' cards
- ☐ Stapler and staples
- ☐ Sticky notes
- ☐ Thumb tacks
- ☐ Whistle
- ☐ Yard stick

Appendix D

Room Essentials to Remember!

- ❑ A box of *Band Aids*
- ❑ A can of air freshener
- ❑ A can of disinfectant
- ❑ A can of *Oops* or similar cleaners for emergencies
- ❑ A canister for lost and used pencils
- ❑ A comfortable stool
- ❑ A good supply of *Post-it* Notes
- ❑ A pop-up container of *Handi Wipes*
- ❑ A small locker mirror attached to a wall or board
- ❑ A small portable erasable white board
- ❑ A working pencil sharpener (don't forget to empty it daily!)
- ❑ A working stapler (remember to refill it!)
- ❑ Assignment & Homework schedule 'due board'
- ❑ Bottle of multi-purpose contact solution
- ❑ Boxes of *Kleenex*
- ❑ Calendar
- ❑ Clock (*behind* students if possible)
- ❑ *Command Strips* (pack or two)
- ❑ Display board for student pictures/work
- ❑ Duct tape
- ❑ Emergency exit diagram
- ❑ Emergency lesson plan (for anyone to teach)
- ❑ Emergency/School phone number list
- ❑ Masking tape
- ❑ Paper towels
- ❑ Posted bell schedule *with Lunch!*
- ❑ Room hall pass or sign-out sheet
- ❑ School Grading Scale
- ❑ *Scotch Tape* & dispenser
- ❑ Sub folder
- ❑ Sufficient board markers/chalk, with erasers
- ❑ Wastebasket (or two!)

Appendix E

Characteristics and Needs of Middle Schoolers[13]

Physical
- Rapid, irregular and unpredictable growth spurts
- Restlessness and impromptu illnesses
- Need opportunities for activity as well as privacy
- Ravenous appetites
- Disturbed by body changes

Intellectual
- Highly curious
- Need opportunity for exploration and extension of knowledge
- Need opportunity to show what they have learned
- Focus on practical rather than theoretical thinking
- Prefer active over passive learning
- Need hands-on and cooperative learning experiences
- Need opportunity for sharing thoughts, feelings and attitudes
- Self-centered
- Developing the ability to think beyond their own skin

Social
- Rebellious toward authority
- Confused by new and unknown things
- Fiercely loyal to their own
- Often aggressive & argumentative
- Need frequent affirmation and approval and the opportunity for expression

Psychological
- Erratic & inconsistent in behavior
- Highly sensitive to criticism /Susceptible to low self-esteem
- Need opportunities for success & recognition
- Moody restless, and self-conscious yet generally optimistic & hopeful
- Searching for identity & peer approval yet in need of adult affirmation

Ethical
- Idealistic /High sense of fairness, and right & wrong
- Reflective and introspective
- Need consistency & direction in what is right and wrong
- Confrontive of moral & ethical questions
- Curious about the essence of life

Appendix F

Characteristics of Gifted and At Risk Middle Schoolers[14]

Gifted/Talented Middle Schoolers

> Avid readers
> Excel in science, math, and literature
> Wide range of interests
> Anxious to try new things
> Seem alert
> Alert and Answer rapidly
> Inquisitive and innovative
> Verbally expressive
> Imaginative in storytelling
> Mature sense of humor
> Like to work alone
> Tend to lose awareness of time
> Self-motivated
> Anxious to complete tasks
> Creative thoughts & expressions
> Problem solvers
> Sensitive to thoughts and feelings of others
> Self-confident
> Dominate groups

At-Risk Middle Schoolers

> Demonstrate academic & achievement gaps
> Inattentive
> Easily distracted
> Short attention spans
> Low self-esteem
> Poor social skills
> Narrow range of interests
> Seek attention in inappropriate ways
> Dependent
> Fear failure
> Lack structure & organization
> Avoid responsibility & independence

Appendix G

Parent Alert Notification

Dear Parent/Guardian:

I need your help. This form is being sent to you to alert you that your son/daughter is experiencing a serious difficulty in Social Studies. Any assistance on your part would be most helpful. Please feel free to contact me if you would like to discuss this matter, *or send feedback on the other side of this form, and return it to me.*

Student: _____Date: _____

Current Social Studies Grade: **Conduct:** *Excellent _____*
     A B C D F   *Satisfactory _____*
                                                    Unsatisfactory _____

The Problem at this time is:

- o   *Low Test Scores _____*
- o   *Failure to Turn in Assignments _____*
- o   *Unexplained Drop in Work Quality _____*
- o   *Inappropriate Talking or Language _____*
- o   *Appears Unmotivated, Unconcerned _____*
- o   *Seems to Not Understand; Confused & Off-task _____*
- o   *Discipline Problem/Refusal to Cooperate _____*

Explanation:

_____

_____

_____

Thank you very much for your concern and assistance in this matter. Our goal is for all students to reach their maximum level of achievement, and I knew you'd want to know about this problem before final grades make it too late to change.

Jerry L. Parks,
Georgetown Middle School

Parent signature_____

How you can be reached _____

Appendix H

When Conferencing with Parents:

- ❏ Keep a positive and professional demeanor at all times.

- ❏ Warmly thank the parent for coming.

- ❏ Keep in mind the parents are generally not teachers and may not view education the same way you do.

- ❏ Arrange the conference setting so parents do not feel on the spot, or 'us against them.'

- ❏ Remember, parents are usually more nervous about conferences than you are. They're on your home turf.

- ❏ Emphasize that everyone desires to do what's best for the child. Seek the parents' help in the matters. Present yourself as an ally – not a foe.

- ❏ Invite both parents wherever this is possible.

- ❏ Check with your guidance office before discussing the student with non-custodial parents, stepparents, etc. Such may not have rights to privacy.

- ❏ Keep a written record of the conference and give one copy to the parents.

- ❏ Do not schedule a conference that will have to be rushed through. Allow adequate time.

- ❏ Schedule a future conference if necessary. Arrange for some type of follow-up.

- ❏ Anticipate questions and have documented records of grades, conduct reports, sample work, etc.

- ❏ Address parents by name, and be sure you have the correct pronunciation.

- ❏ Don't assume every student has the typical nuclear family. Anticipate surprises.

- ❏ Listen to what the parent has to say.

- ❏ Try to start off and end on a positive note – address strengths and weaknesses. Every child has both.

- ❑ Have a tough skin—don't take things personally.

- ❑ Remember the student's version and the truth are often not the same.

- ❑ If the parent brings up an issue that is uncomfortable, they must believe it's a problem.

- ❑ Make sure you really *listen*, and look them in the eye.

- ❑ Do not work on other things in the presence of a parent. Appear as though the conference is as important to you as it obviously is to them.

- ❑ Make sure the parent is aware of any school or classroom policy to be enforced.

- ❑ Ask if possibly there are extenuating circumstances, which might be affecting the child.

- ❑ Ask for the child to attend the last part of the conference so they can see you and the parents are acting as a united front, and can understand the plan of action also.

- ❑ Focus on specific strategies and solutions rather than emphasizing the problem.

- ❑ Deal in specifics. Do not waste your time, or the parents', in vague generalities. That is not why they came.

- ❑ Have all behavior issues documented—with specifics, not just generalities.

- ❑ Bring any documentation you are wanting to discuss (test papers, etc.).

- ❑ If you aren't understanding what the parent is talking about—stop them and ask them make it clear.

- ❑ Do not discuss any other students, nor use their names or papers as examples.

- ❑ Speak in parent language—not educational techno-jargon. Parents will not be impressed.

- ❑ When in doubt as to whether to say something or not, *don't*. Never miss an opportunity to keep your mouth shut.

❏ Keep all the papers you are given.

❏ Keep the meeting moving and discussions on task in a polite manner.

❏ Do not work on other material in front of the parent.

❏ End the meeting on a positive note and thank the parent for coming.

Questions you may want to discuss:

- What are the child's past school experiences?

- Are there any family issues that should be discussed?

- How does the child feel about school in general?

- How does the child seem to learn best?

- Are there concerns about the company the child is keeping?

- Are there any peer conflicts at this time?

- What are the child's study habits at home?

- What is the parent's homework policy at home?

- Which behavior concerns the parent most?

- Does the parent set a required study time at home whether the child says they have homework or not? (They can always *read.*)

Appendix I

First Open House for Parents[15]

Chicken Soup for Parenting:
"HELP! I woke up and my child was in middle school!"

Dear Mom and Dad: the bad news is—*you* have to survive middle school *too!* The good news is—here are some research-based and eminently practical suggestions to make sure your middle schooler is successful. Employ (and *enjoy!*) each of these help tips written specifically for *you*—the parents of a middle schooler. Remember—when you help your child, you are helping your child's teacher also!

"The job of a teacher is not to fill a bucket, but to light a fire."

✓ **Check agenda books and notebooks** daily, and **please check your child's grades!** It has been my experience that if he or she cannot show their grades to you, *90% of the time they are failing.* All grades and graded papers are kept in these two books. **PLEASE help me help them**—check daily! Find playful ways to check up on assignments. Do a few problems together, show them how to correct mistakes, and then *let your child work alone.* Even if you feel you can't help with homework—if nothing else—you can help with organization skills, which will eventually help everything else!

✓ **Homework. Ten minutes per night multiplied by the grade level** is the most efficient (total) time to be allotted for homework. Help set up a consistent, organized *schedule* and *place* for homework to be done–with supplies and good lighting. Middle Schoolers thrive on routine. Help establish one. (*Homework is independent, unmonitored practice*!)

✓ Also regarding homework, if your child is practicing a *skill*, ask him/her to tell you what's easy, what's hard, and **how they are** *going to improve.* If your child is doing a *project*, ask them **what knowledge they are** *applying* in the project. If they cannot answer these questions, the homework is useless—something is wrong—and you probably need to find out what it is.

✓ Homework should be considered a **'quiet time'** in which you are available to help. Nevertheless, when bedtime comes, stop your child from homework—even if the homework is not done. Sufficient sleep is second only to nutrition & nurture in importance for growth in teens. *Suggestion:* **Have them set out all books and papers the night before**, so they won't be rushed into forgetting things in the morning.

✓ Whenever possible, **connect homework to family activities** (math to pricing items, social studies to upcoming TV documentaries and family trips, language arts to films, newspaper and magazine readings, etc.) *This increases the quality of learning logarithmically*!

✓ Reward positive accomplishments (an agenda book completely filled in, perfect papers, etc.) on a *weekly* basis. **An ounce of *positive feedback* is worth more than a pound of criticism**. (Unfortunately, however, it won't be remembered nearly as long.) A little goes a long way, and middle schoolers love routine.

✓ Keep a scrapbook or memory box of their middle school years. **Your child really will look back upon these years as the most special**. By the time high school rolls around, the opportunity to create something so sweet will be gone forever.

✓ Ask your child to teach you at least three new things they learned each day! *Listening* is one of the greatest—and most neglected—skills of parenting. Discuss daily school activities each evening! **Look your child in the eye and *really* listen!**

✓ Plan at least one visit to *each* of your child's classes during the year, and attend school functions as often as you are able. As a general rule— *parents who care are parents who are there!*

✓ Be tolerant of a low score every once in a while, but never, ***never* accept a 'zero'** without finding out why. We all have off days, but a zero is either a careless attitude or a lesson unlearned, and both are disastrous to academic averages and character development!

✓ *Be a parent—not a friend. Lay down firm rules and consequences at home, and hold your child accountable. At first they'll complain, soon they'll appreciate it, and when they mature, they will thank you for the rest of their lives. **Remember—even though you can't be a perfect parent, you can still be a good one! "Dare to Care!"***

Appendix J

Introducing 'Me'! (Icebreaker Activity)

(SAMPLE QUESTIONS—Choose several, not all, to ask students to complete.)

A friend is:

A goal in life I have is:

A good student:

A good teacher:

Another age I'd like to be is:

I learn best when:

I really feel good when:

I worry most about:

I would like to tell my family:

I would like to tell my friends:

I would like to tell my teachers:

If I had a role model, it would be:

My favorite leisure-time activity:

One thing I do well is:

One thing I'd like my parents to know:

One thing I'd like teachers to know:

Someday, I'd like to be:

The best thing about my age is:

The best thing about my gender is:

The best thing about school is:

The last thing that made me feel really bad was:

The most important person ever born was:

The most important person I've ever known was:

The worst thing about my gender is:

The worst thing about school is:

When I need to feel better, I:

When I think of the future:

Appendix K

Bloom's Taxonomy

Level I: Knowledge—to learn and bring to mind information.

Memory recall of basic facts and answers.

Prompts: *who, what, list, find, match, define, where, label, name, show, recall, omit, count, locate, trace, underline, record, pick, quote, choose, fill-in, identify, tell, match*

Important for foundational support.
Developed through practice and repetition.

❑ The student absorbs, remembers recognizes, recalls, and responds. *"Where are pyramids located?"*

Demonstrators: vocabulary lists, workbook activities, quizzes

Level II: Comprehension—to understand and grasp the meaning of information.

Demonstration of facts by interpretation (meaning) or description.

Prompts: *rephrase, compare, contrast, explain why, summarize, illustrate, outline, show, associate, describe, define, reword, simplify, exemplify, change, interpret*

Requires an extension of knowledge, or basic use of an idea.
Directed toward a specific *action* or *communication.*

❑ The student translates or interprets, but does not relate information to other material. *"Contrast the differences between Egyptian and Mesoamerican pyramids."*

Demonstrators: drawings, diagrams

Level III: Application—to use learned material in a new and specific situation.

Problem-solving by transferring and applying previous information to that which is new or different.

Prompts: *apply, utilize, choose, interview, solve, model, for example, develop, organize, predict, identify, determine, modify, if, utilize, transfer, suppose, participate, distinguish, derive*

Requires not merely use of learned material, but use in a new way. Recognize a problem & decide from given choices what will solve it.

❑ The student solves or constructs in new situations using principles, concepts, or theories. *"Give an example of modern technology that might have made pyramid building easier in the ancient world."*

Demonstrators: Recipes, models, artwork, demonstration

Level IV: Analysis—to break down info in order to understand organizational structure.

Examining and breaking down information to identify cause. Infer and support generalizations produced.

Prompts: *analyze, infer, categorize, simplify, conclude, examine, assume, relate, justify, criticize, detect, diagram, when would, discriminate, transform, sort, survey, group, inspect, dissect, differentiate, specify*

Requires the learner to: 'read between the lines,' find subtle cues, and study organization patterns.

❑ The student divides information into component elements. *"In your opinion, why do cultures feel the need to build such great structures?"*

Demonstrators: Advanced writing and reasoning expression

Level V: Synthesis—to reformulate the component parts together into a new whole.

Compiling and combining elements in a new pattern, or propose alternative solutions.

Prompts: *estimate, construct, imagine, compose, solve, improve, propose how, design, arrange, extend, devise, formulate, integrate, suppose, revise, pretend, invent, predict*

> Involves careful thought of a previous creation.
> Requires the reverse intellectual process from analysis.
> Recognizes a problem and proposes ideas / materials, to solve it.

> ❏ The student reforms a (new) whole and can apply and analyze it. *"Pretend you were spending one day in either ancient pyramid-building culture. Write one entry in your journal on your feelings as you watched the ancient pyramid builders at work."*

Demonstrators: Inventions, songs, poems, advertisements

Level VI: Evaluation—to judge the value of info against criteria for a given purpose.

Reflect upon and make recommendations of material.

Prompts: *appraise, argue, critique, test, verify, validate, interpret, measure, evaluate, defend, support, recommend, rank, grade, judge whether, determine, justify, assess, prioritize*

> Learner judges through careful thought and application of a criterion, which they generate and justify, as relevant.

> ❏ Student determines value according to purpose and against a criterion.
> *"Should the ancient pyramids be preserved as tourist attractions, or removed for land reclamation and farming? Justify your position."*

Demonstrators: Editorials, critiques, rating scales, debates

Note: Students who can *analyze, synthesize,* and *evaluate* become more effective thinkers.

Appendix L

Addressing the Multiple Intelligences

Linguistic/Verbal *(Attorneys, Authors, Ministers, Sales!)*
"Just give me the words, man—I think in words!"

Share ideas	Use flash cards
Debate an issue	Study etymology
Assign a presentation	Emphasize vocabulary

Involve creative reading, writing, and storytelling!
Use word association and Jeopardy-type games
Utilize puns, similes, metaphors, and limericks

Spatial/Visual *(Artists, Interior decorators, Architects, Photographers!)*
"If I can see it, I can…"

Make a collage	Show videos
Create a brochure	Involve a chart or map
Design a poster	Utilize their imagination
Emphasize color and perspective	Illustrate a story
Use pictures and photos	

Use diagramming and visualization scenarios

Logical/Mathematical *(Accountants, Scientists, Computer programmers, Detectives!)*
"I think in the abstract, and I'm a problem-solver!"

Perform experiments	Solve a dilemma
Design a graph or timeline or puzzle	Use a calculator
Create a code or symbol	Interpret data
Utilize compare and contrast	Utilize prediction

Evaluate an idea, decision, video, or book
Utilize prediction of consequences
Use syllogisms and analogies

Musical/Rhythmic *(Musicians, Composers!)*
"If I can hear it, I can…"

Sing a song	Analyze a commercial
Write a jingle	Play background music
Research a Rocker!	Make up a rap song

Utilize videotaping and multimedia opportunities

Interpersonal (Politicians, Teachers, Actors!)
"Let's do it together!"

Have group presentations
Debate in pairs
Make rows into teams!
Conduct interviews and surveys
Present group problem-solving activities
Utilize E-mail and telephone activities
Use cooperative learning and partnering paradigms

Emphasize taking turns
Role-play!
Establish group goals
Let students teach

Intrapersonal (Theologians, Philosophers, Psychologists!)
"Can I just think about this awhile?"

Do self-study quizzes and inventories
Allow sustained silent reading
Reflect and write about issues and events
Assign individualized projects and independent study
Have students personalize assignments, scenarios, events, etc.

Assign a journal
Assign an opinion paper

Bodily/Kinesthetic (Athletes, Surgeons, Dancers, Carpenters!)
"Let's get down and DO it, baby!"

Assign a project or experiment
Involve an outdoor activity
Play a charade or pantomime game
Role-play an event
Work with manipulatives
Relate learning to sports

Perform a play
Take field trips

Naturalistic (Ecologists, Zoologists!)
"If we can GO, I'll GROW!"

Utilize pictures and photos
Involve outdoor activities
Have students sort, categorize and classify
Use collection, organization, and reporting activities

Go on a hike
Take a field trip

Appendix M

Student Report Form
7th Grade Team

Student Name _____

Teacher _____   **Date** _____

Subject _____ **Period** _____

Due to circumstances, I cannot attend this meeting. Here is a summary of the student's performance in my class. Please feel free to contact me if you have any questions.

Grades:

Behavior:

Concerns:

Recommendations:

Teacher signature _____ **Date** _____

Appendix N

Ideas for Spicing Up Your Teaching Instruction!
(Authentic/Differentiated Instruction)

Authentic assessment connects learning to real-world experience. It includes: a portfolio of student work, a performance to be observed, and a product to be displayed or filed.

- ❑ Brainstorm activity
- ❑ Build a model
- ❑ Cell phone conversation with an imaginary friend or famous character
- ❑ Class discussions
- ❑ Cooperative learning
- ❑ Debates
- ❑ Diagrams
- ❑ Displays
- ❑ Drama or simulations
- ❑ Essay
- ❑ Experiments
- ❑ Fold-a-books
- ❑ Game activity
- ❑ Group discussions
- ❑ Guest speakers
- ❑ Homework lottery
- ❑ Interpretations
- ❑ Interviews
- ❑ Jeopardy review
- ❑ Museum/exhibit
- ❑ Oral presentations
- ❑ Pamphlet
- ❑ Plays
- ❑ Podcasts/blogs
- ❑ Portfolios
- ❑ PowerPoint Presentations
- ❑ Projects
- ❑ Questionnaires
- ❑ Role-play
- ❑ Scrapbooks
- ❑ Simulations
- ❑ Slideshows
- ❑ Storyboards
- ❑ Surveys
- ❑ Videos
- ❑ Webpage/Webquests

Appendix O

The A+ Teacher: Characteristics of the Best Classroom Teachers, and What They Do On a Regular Basis[16]

- A+ teachers are approachable, affirming, and demonstrate warmth
- A+ teachers are flexible, spontaneous, and utilize teachable moments
- A+ teachers are optimistic and generally self-confident
- A+ teachers can see things from their students' perspective
- A+ teachers challenge, and stimulate critical thinking
- A+ teachers communicate with parents regularly
- A+ teachers compliment often
- A+ teachers connect lessons to life
- A+ teachers continually communicate realistic high expectations
- A+ teachers continually learn from mistakes and hone their skills
- A+ teachers continually monitor and assess
- A+ teachers dare to be creative
- A+ teachers do not overcorrect misbehavior, intimidate, or embarrass
- A+ teachers empathize and show sensitivity
- A+ teachers encourage and practice reflection
- A+ teachers encourage questions and admit it when they don't know
- A+ teachers encourage through correction
- A+ teachers establish routines and order
- A+ teachers exhibit a contagious sense of humor
- A+ teachers genuinely listen to their students
- A+ teachers grow professionally, and share what they learn with peers
- A+ teachers have a student-friendly, inviting room
- A+ teachers incorporate success-building behavior into their teaching
- A+ teachers learn their students' names
- A+ teachers leave comments on graded papers
- A+ teachers manage rather than simply control a classroom

- A+ teachers practice time management and keep their students on task
- A+ teachers praise genuinely
- A+ teachers provide opportunity for extra help
- A+ teachers show awareness of middle schoolers' developmental needs
- A+ teachers show enthusiasm for teaching through energy and animation
- A+ teachers smile often, and show a passion for teaching
- A+ teachers teach through discovery and exploration
- A+ teachers teach with clarity in the content they present
- A+ teachers vary teaching and instructional strategies

Appendix P

The D- Teacher: Characteristics of What Poorly Performing Teachers Do On a Regular Basis"

- D- teachers use sarcasm and shame to win power struggles
- D- teachers embarrass and ridicule as a form of punishment
- D- teachers never learn their students' names
- D- teachers are disorganized, and their students know it
- D- teachers use insensitive language toward various culture groups
- D- teachers have difficulty working with peers and colleagues
- D- teachers have inadequate knowledge of how kids grow and develop
- D- teachers reward inappropriate behavior
- D- teachers spend inordinate time trying to be popular
- D- teachers teach in a monotone, and with little variety of style
- D- teachers exhibit limited knowledge of the subject matter they teach
- D- teachers exhibit little preparation and keep regular hours at all times
- D- teachers show favoritism and forget the bottom half of the class
- D- teachers scold and scream in an effort to be effective

Appendix Q

Sample Lesson Plan

Writing a Feature Article
"The Democratic Process and the Freedoms We Enjoy"
(As a required portfolio writing entry)

Created by: Jerry L. Parks, Social Studies-7,
Georgetown Middle School, Georgetown, KY
Subject/Grade level: Social Studies 7

Overview:
Students will understand how the democratic process is a foundational concept in America and how our representative form of government is a by-product of the search for freedom. *Academic Expectations: 2.14, 2.15, 2.16, and 2.19 (Kentucky Core Content)*

Skill:
Students will learn how one patriot, Jessica Lynch, changed her perception of the freedoms we enjoy due to her service in Iraq, and how to formulate their own feature article (portfolio piece) based upon this exemplar.

Assignment:
Students will write a feature article on *"Why I'm glad I'm an American"*

Expectations:
Students will better understand the cost of freedom, and the Pledge to our flag.

Materials needed:
      1. Article on the pledge of allegiance by Jessica Lynch
      2. Pencil and paper for students

Room modifications or equipment needed: None

Time Allotment: 2-3 class periods

Terms/Concepts to Learn or Review:

Democracy	Monarchy
Republic	Allegiance
Dictatorship	Indivisible

Homework to Assign:

Students will complete the task by the following school day.

Preparation and Standards Addressed:

1. Students will understand the concept of democracy.
2. Students will understand the concept of representative government and how it differs from democracy.
3. Students will have studied the contrast between these government forms and the dynastic dictatorships of ancient Egypt and kingships of Sumer.
4. Students will be familiar with, and experienced in, composing a (required) portfolio entry.
5. Students will be familiar with the pledge of allegiance to our flag.

Activity:

➢ Discuss with students the requirement of portfolio entries from social studies.
➢ Discuss with students the pledge of allegiance and Jessica Lynch.
➢ Discuss with students the importance of freedom and the democratic process.
➢ Read Jessica Lynch's *"What the Pledge Means to Me" (Parade, 11/16/03).*
➢ Discuss with students the thoughts stimulated by the article and have them brainstorm possible inclusions for the article, such as *democracy, freedoms, worship, equality, responsibilities, rights, capitalism,* etc.
➢ Challenge students to understand the concept of a feature article (stressing *audience*, etc.).
➢ Discuss and begin the assignment (writing a feature article), which should be completed as homework. Students should begin the process in class and be directed and redirected as necessary.

Follow-up activity:

Students discuss the feature-writing process and differing views on why each chose the subject they chose. Students will be given the opportunity to share their feature article with the class and stimulate discussion on what made each a successful writing piece.

Review for Emphasis:

Discuss with the students how and why different cultures around the world have differing views of freedom, why the democratic process allows the most benefit to the citizen, and the responsibilities and sacrifices necessary to maintain such a culture.

Evaluation & Assessment:

Students will be evaluated according to a teacher-created rubric.

Appendix R

The 'Mastery Principle' of a Successful Lesson Plan!

Here is everything college, experience, and professional development can teach you about teaching, condensed into seven simple tidbits! Fine tune, practice, and perfect these, and you will be the best teacher you can be. **Make sure your lessons are**:

M—*multiple intelligences addressed.* Does my lesson create a broad opportunity for learning by recognizing and addressing the diversity of learning styles among my students?

A—*application centered.* Does my lesson provide for my students to be able to apply the learning to their personal, social, cultural, or global concerns?

S—*standards based.* Does my lesson stem from the state and national standards in my subject area and cover the content I am supposed to be teaching?

T—*testing and assessment geared.* Does my lesson link into a measurable, valid, and cumulative assessment for my students to demonstrate what they have learned in a variety of ways?

E—*engagingly presented.* Does my lesson capture the interest of my students and challenge them into forced questioning, goal setting, and critical thinking skills?

R—*resource friendly.* Does my lesson utilize diverse resource materials extending beyond the textbook, such as other people, interdisciplinary units, activities, technology, the community, and practical lessons from everyday life?

Y—*youth focused.* Does my lesson focus on the needs of my students—considering their age, prior knowledge, and experiences? Does the lesson allow more for student investigation rather than being teacher—oriented?

Appendix S

Your First Observation & Teacher Evaluation

The Pre-conference:

✓ Be sure lesson plans contain the goals and standards you must address.
✓ Ask questions about anything you do not understand about the process.
✓ Be familiar with the forms, and the criteria for your evaluation.
✓ Inform the evaluator of any extenuating circumstances that may take place during the evaluation.

During the evaluation:

✓ Dress comfortably but appropriately.
✓ Be yourself. There are no perfect teachers, or behavior management plans.
✓ Make sure your room is clean.
✓ Prepare ahead of time where you want the evaluator to sit, and any class handouts you want them to have.
✓ Thank the evaluator for coming. Explain to students why they're there.
✓ Relax. Smile! Act like you enjoy your job!
✓ Review.
✓ Call students by names.
✓ Continually assess through questioning.
✓ Address teachable moments.
✓ Encourage, redirect, and deliver positive feedback.
✓ Do not stand still. Circulate among the students. 'Stir the soup!'
✓ Anticipate and prepare for interruptions – they will happen!
✓ Remember short attention spans.
✓ Prepare students for the next lesson.

The Post-conference

✓ Take a notepad.
✓ Thank the evaluator for coming.
✓ Explain any circumstances that you feel need explanation.
✓ Listen carefully to any criticisms.
✓ Do not be afraid to ask for suggestions, and write them down.
✓ Sign the form. Keep a copy.
✓ Plan the next evaluation if one is required.

Appendix T

Important Documents to Keep!

❑ A current copy of your teaching certificate and school district contract

❑ A current list of any professional development you've earned (dated and described)

❑ A list of your core content or National/State Standards in your subject area

❑ Copies of all your past and current teaching evaluations/observations, any honors, commendations, accomplishments, and your current salary schedule.

❑ Letters from parents, the community, and significant notes from students

❑ Summary notes from parent conferences or administrator conferences

❑ The school, school board, or county employee policy manual or code of ethics

❑ Parent contact forms

❑ Field trip forms

❑ Copy of conduct or discipline reports filed

❑ IEP's and adaptations for current students

❑ Receipts for any monies turned in

❑ Copies of Professional Development verification

Appendix U

Substitute Teacher Form

Date:

Dear Substitute:

Thank you very much for coming today!

"If you need help ask _____ *"*

- ❏ Emergency procedures/fire drills/building map:

- ❏ Medical issues:

- ❏ Supplies for classroom: (books, handouts, homework boxes, pencils, etc.)

- ❏ Seating charts:

- ❏ Non-teaching duties/personal responsibilities:

- ❏ Specific instructions for special classes/children:

- ❏ General classroom expectations/consequences:

- ❏ Lunch schedule/procedure:

- ❏ Computer/media rules:

- ❏ Daily school activities/possible interruptions:

- ❏ Attendance forms/procedures:

- ❏ Hall passes/procedures:

- ❏ Daily schedule:

- ❏ Sponge (leftover time) activities:

- ❏ Dismissal (bus) procedures/times:

Final note: Before the last class leaves, please make sure they straighten all rows and pick up all stuff on floor. Thanks for coming!

Appendix V

Sample Collaborative Teacher Information Letter

Dear collaboration teacher:

I am looking forward to working with you this year! In order to get the year off to a good start, here are some things that will help me a great deal. I realize you cannot do all of these every time you are here, but I would appreciate your assistance as much as possible.

o Be here. That is the most important thing you can do.

o Make sure the students know you are here for ALL of them. This is very important in continuing class unity.

o Help me with attendance. If you are here during homeroom, this is especially important.

o Help with discipline. Kids need to see and understand your authority.

o Please help me 'stir the room'. By this I mean we need to walk around the room at regular intervals and KEEP KIDS ON TASK. I have found that the kids pay attention when they know their teachers are paying attention.

o Volunteer information (of any kind). Please don't wait to be asked. The kids need to see you as a teacher just as they do me. I am not the least bit offended when you jump right in with comments, suggestions, reminders, etc.

o Help me clarify. Sometimes your ability to restate the obvious will benefit the kids understanding.

o Assist with board work. Feel free to write whatever supplementary notes you feel necessary on the board. My space is your space.

o Help me grade assignments. If you will take care of your kids' grading and grades, I would very much appreciate it. The standards you set for many of your students will probably differ from mine.

o Remind me of special IEP requirements I may need to address.

This is a TEAM effort, and I would appreciate all the assistance you can offer. Thank you!

Appendix W

End of the Year Checklist!
(I thought this day would never come!)

- o   Are all book and room repair requests turned in?
- o   Are all book damage fees accounted for?
- o   Are all library books that were in my room returned?
- o   Are all textbooks collected?
- o   Are my boards cleaned and ready for next year?
- o   Are my grades turned in?
- o   Did I complete book/room /AV inventory?
- o   Did I delete all old emails, documents and programs I won't need?
- o   Did I set my thermostat for summer?
- o   Did I unplug my computer and AV equipment?
- o   Did I unplug (for defrost) my room fridge?
- o   Do I have all plants and creatures taken care of for summer?
- o   Have all leftover report cards been turned in?
- o   Have I backed up all computer files (take home important ones)?
- o   Have I left a room-plan map for custodians waxing my floor?
- o   Have I left my summer contact number and address?
- o   Have I prepared next year's supply list?
- o   Have I returned all required AV equipment?
- o   Have I thanked my team—especially my team leader?
- o   Have I thrown out all junk and placed canisters for pick-up?
- o   Have I turned in all required paperwork?
- o   Have I turned in my Professional Development plan?
- o   Is my bulletin board ready to go?
- o   Did I check and clean out any lockers I need to?
- o   Did I collect locks and attach combinations?
- o   Did I turn in any unclaimed awards or report cards?
- o   Have I turned in all monies I may have collected?
- o   Did I thank all the volunteers to my classroom this year?
- o   Have I put a summer message on my website?

Appendix X

Ten Commandments on Becoming the Poorest Middle School Teacher You Can Be

   I. Thou shalt compare students with peers (in classes, and in families).

  II. Thou shalt sit at thy desk at all times, talk on thy cell phone, text thy friends, and strive to simply keep your students busy.

 III. Thou shalt treat thy students as they treat thee, and remember that one negative comment deserves another.

  IV. Thou shalt view thy students' parents as the enemy at all times.

   V. Thou shalt regard tests as challenges which few students should be able to conquer—a contest between you and them, where only one can be the winner.

  VI. Thou shalt designate one day per week as 'fun time' .

 VII. Thou shalt never allow thy students to become 'people' in thine estimation. Neither shalt thy listen to them or care about their interests or concerns.

VIII. Thou shalt NEVER admit fault.

  IX. Thou shalt be amongst the first to hear the newest rumors and shalt share what thou hast heard amongst any who will listen.

   X. Never admit thou dost not know – to students, parents, or colleagues. Thou shalt never seek advice or help from older colleagues.

Appendix Y

Parks' Ponderables for Students

I. Life isn't fair. Get used to it.

II. The real world won't care about you nearly as much as your parents and teachers do right now. Appreciate it. Don't cop an attitude.

III. If you think teachers are tough, wait till you get a boss someday!

IV. Don't blame others for your mistakes. Taking more responsibility makes you look less like a child.

V. Teachers are not responsible for ensuring that you have fun. They *are* responsible to make sure you learn. Don't complain. There are worse places you could be.

VI. Your reputation is your most important possession. Cheaters are losers— remember that.

VII. TV bears no resemblance to the real world. Don't think that life will always entertain you, or that its problems are neatly resolved in half hour segments.

VIII. How you speak and present yourself is the *first* impression you will make on others. If you do it poorly, it may also be the *last* impression you make on a prospective employer when you interview someday.

IX. Things are not true because teachers tell you. We tell you because they're true. Trust us—we have your best interest at heart.

X. You generally receive the same respect you give, so use your brain before you exercise your mouth.

XI. Life isn't divided into grading periods, nor does it give you summers off. Stop complaining about school and enjoy the ride while you can.

XII. Take advantage of opportunities. Some, you will only get once.

XIII. Unlike school, life doesn't give you as many chances as you need to get everything right. *Think* before you do or say something that might affect the rest of your life.

XIV. Honor your parents and strive to be *better* than they are. They brought you up. Don't let them down.

XV. Never put off till tomorrow what *needs* to be done today.

Appendix Z

Great Websites for Teachers!

http://www.educationworld.com/--this site calls itself 'The Educator's Best Friend'. With all the helpful material for instructors, it just might be!

http://www.disciplinehelp.com/teacher/--a very interesting site that presents teachers with suggestions of dealing with every time of discipline behavior.

http://abcteach.com/--this is a great site for timesaving tips for teachers.
http://ask.com/--a great site for asking virtually any question!

http://atozteacherstuff.com/--a virtually unlimited source of lesson plans, tips & tools.

http://homeworkspot.com/middle/--contains many sites and references for teachers

http://puzzlemaker.school.discovery.com/--indispensible source of free word search, puzzle and maze makers which teachers can modify!

http://resumes-for-teachers.com/--need a resume or writing service? This site focuses on all things to do with education including job search resources.

http://sitesforteachers.com/index.html--there's no end to the list of clipart, pictures, lessons, and innumerable other resources for teachers.

http://teachingtreasures.com.au/-- teaching tools, resources, games, etc.

http://www.braingle.com/-- over 20,000 brainteasers, riddles, logic problems, quizzes and mind puzzles

http://www.creativeteachingsite.com/--this site focuses on improving your creative teaching styles

http://www.edhelper.com/--another site for creating worksheets, puzzles, thematic units

http://www.etymonline.com/--middle schoolers love etymology. This site will help you locate the origin of words

http://www.freakyfreddies.com/teacher.htm--another of those sites that list compendium of teaching resources teachers can procure http://graphjam.com/-- a creative site for teachers to make graphs of virtually anything. Challenge and fascinate your students while teaching them to visually analyze

http://www.inspiringteachers.com/-- a community of educators networking for mutual growth and support in the teaching profession.

http://www.lessonplansearch.com/--1500 lesson plans arranged by subject!

http://www.lessonplanspage.com/--lesson plans, plus articles, blogs and games.

http://www.kodakgallery.com/Welcome.jsp--free photo sharing website the kids love to visit. Password protected.

http://www.puzzledepot.com/cwe/index.shtml--challenges your brain with free puzzles, Shockwave and Flash games, crosswords, logic games, IQ tests, trivia games and contests for prizes.

http://www.quotesandsayings.com/-- this is a pop-up free resource offering quotes, quotations and sayings organized by subject and by author.

http://www.refdesk.com/--just about anything that can be referenced is here!

http://www.school-clip-art.com/--when you need free clip art for handouts or brochures, this is the place to go.

http://www.schoolnotes.com/40324/jparks.html--personalize your own location for your students to find your homework. Schoolnotes is one of the best!

http://www.sde.com/index.asp-- *Staff Development for Educators* is a wonderful site for instructing teachers on how to put theory into practice. (Great site for differentiated instruction!)

http://www.teacherplanet.com/calendar/calendar.php?op=cal&month=6&year=2010--lesson plans, awards, worksheets, freebees—you need it—it's here!

http://www.teachingheart.net/newteacher.html--cozy and helpful site for new teachers. Instructions on setting up your room, doing bulletin boards, etc.

http://www.theteacherscorner.net/--really nice site for worksheets, teacher tools, grants, and thematic units.

http://www.paperrater.com/--ever wonder if your students are plagiarizing?

Appendix AA

Characteristics of Teaching Excellence

The movie *Dead Poet's Society* features Robin Williams as an instructor at a small college-prep New England school for boys. Williams is an excellent example of a master teacher. His characteristics of good teaching are a model for all new and veteran teachers. He:

1. Was well-prepared in the knowledge of his content.

2. Inspired his students by his love not just for them—but also for his subject.

3. Called each student by name, and continually showed each of them respect.

4. Recognized the strength of each of his students, and utilized it.

5. Recognized the weaknesses of his students, and figured out a creative way to address that weakness. In doing so he never ridiculed or embarrassed.

6. Was willing to take a chance in doing something completely different, or in a novel manner.

7. Made a unique first impression on day one!

8. Maintained a sense of humor that kept an atmosphere in his classroom which was conducive to learning.

9. Often surprised his students with activities and styles they could not expect.

10. Taught beyond the classroom, utilizing space beyond the four walls.

11. Forced his students to think for themselves, and come to their own conclusions.

12. Was creative, and sought to become what the typical teacher wasn't!

13. Anticipated his students' questions, thoughts, and opinions.

14. Appealed to his students' curiosity, motivating his students to learn in spite of themselves!

15. Allowed students to organize themselves, and figure things out on their own.

16. Utilized all the space within his classroom (from books, to desks, to lights), and much of it in a unique and memorable way.

17. Knew when not to pressure a student's weakness, and simply left him with encouragement.

18. Encouraged at every opportunity, and gently 'forced' his students to take a chance and realize their own ability for success.

19. Brought more good out of his students than even they thought could be there!

20. Turned negative scenarios into positive learning and modeling experiences, never letting his students feel he'd lost control.

21. Made his lessons unforgettable, knowing how to teach through performance rather than by mere lecture.

22. Corrected his students with dignity and appropriate discipline. He was firm without becoming punitive.

23. Left an impression regarding life, character, and learning which followed his students far beyond the classroom.

24. Had an open-door policy to listen to concerns, but always supported his students' parents.

25. Kept a safe distance from his student's private lives.

Appendix BB

Summation of Standards: The WOW (Working on the Work) Classroom[1]

Working on the Work by Phillip Schlechty is an outline for improving student performance by improving the quality of schoolwork. Schlechty offers 12 standards for achieving this. The standards are summarized below.

❑ **Standard 1:** WOW classes are highly engaged, and students are authentically challenged academically.

❑ **Standard 2:** WOW schools allow parents, teachers, and administrators to all have a stake in the learning process of students.

❑ **Standard 3:** WOW schools have teachers and administrators with a clear and consistent understanding of precisely what students are expected to know.

❑ **Standard 4:** WOW schools ensure that all media and text material are age-appropriate and organized in a way to appeal to students.

❑ **Standard 5:** WOW schools ensure that all assignments and activities are linked to student interest and value.

❑ **Standard 6:** WOW schools ensure that students understand the standards by which all their work will be evaluated.

❑ **Standard 7:** WOW classrooms are an environment of mutual respect, and a physically and psychologically safe environment where success is expected and failure is understood.

❑ **Standard 8:** WOW schools understand that student achievement is to be shared beyond the classroom.

❑ **Standard 9:** WOW schools ensure that students are given opportunity to work with adults and other peers in a cooperative learning environment.

❑ **Standard 10:** WOW schools ensure that student performances are wide and varied, and that a wide variety of technology is employed.

❑ **Standard 11:** WOW schools ensure that students are required to learn according to set standards, but that they are allowed choice and options in the learning process.

❑ **Standard 12:** WOW schools ensure that students see meaning and significance in what they are taught.

Appendix CC

Presenting the Lesson

There are no set rules on presenting a lesson to middle schoolers, and the format will vary according to subject area. The important aspects of any lesson presentation, however, should consist of basic and important tenets. These are included in the follow flow-sample using the easy-to-remember acronym: *teacher*.

Transition. Begin by transitioning from the previous less, homework, etc. Correct any misunderstandings, and discuss what was to be learned.

Engagement. Allow middle schoolers to use their senses through engagement. Introduce new material through a story, quote, illustration, visual, etc. Be creative. Capture their attention.

Activation. Activate higher-order learning skills through whole-class problem-solving, or presenting a dilemma which they must think and solve. This is a great way to create interest in new material.

Challenge. Have students (individually) do an activity applying or using new material. It can be hands-on, or even a small-group activity. Reach your kinesthetic learners.

Homework. Have students further apply and synthesize what new material they've learned through practice. Begin the assignment in class.

Expectation. Make sure students know exactly what is expected of them regarding the homework, how it will be assessed, and what they should have learned today in order to use utilize such knowledge.

Review. Reinforce one final time the highlights of the new material presented. For example, have students identify 3 aspects of the learned material as an exit ticket.

Bibliography

References for suggested reading

Armstrong, Coleen, (2009). *The Truth About Teaching.* **Jossey-Bass Publishers**

Averitt, Angela, (2008). *Middle School Classroom Prescription for Success.* Best Way Publishers

Bloom, B.S., Engelhart, M.D., Furst, E.J., Hill, W.H., & Kratwohl, D.R. (1956). *Taxonomy of Educational Objectives: Cognitive Domain, Handbook 1.* New York: David McKay.

Carlson, Richard, (1999). *A Don't Sweat the Small Stuff Treasury: A Special Selection for Teachers.* **Hyperion Press**

Clark, Ron, (2204). *The Essential 55 Workbook.* Hyperion Press

Cushman, Kathleen, & Rogers, Laura. (2008) *Fires In the Middle School Bathroom.* The New Press

Forte, Imogene, and Schurr, Sandra, (1993). *The Definitive Middle School Guide.* Incentive Publications

Gardner, H., (1999). *Intelligence Re-framed: Multiple Intelligences for the 21st Century.* New York: Basic Books

Heidemann, S., & Hewitt, D., (1992). *Pathways to Play.* St. Paul, MN: Redleaf Press.

Hendricks, Howard, (2003). *Teaching to Change Lives.* Multnomah Books.

Howe, Randy, (2007). *First Year Teacher.* **Kaplan Press.**

Kelley, Melissa, (2010). *The Everything New Teacher Book.* Adams Media

Lemov, Doug, (2010). *Teaching Like a Champion.* **Jossey-Bass Publishers.**

Marzano, Robert, Pickering, Deborah, Pollock, Jane, (2001). *Classroom Instruction that Works.* Alexandria, VA: ASCD Publications.

Parks, Jerry, (2007) *Help! My Child is Starting Middle School!* Weekly Reader Teacher's Press Publishers

Partin, Ronald L., (2009). *The Classroom Teacher's Survival Guide.* **Jossey-Bass Publishers**

Payne, Ruby, (2005). *A Framework for Understating Poverty.* Aha Press, Inc.

Purkey, W. W., & Novak, J., (1996). <u>Inviting School Success</u>. **New York: Wadsworth Publishing Co.**

Scavone, Natalie, (2003). *National Board Certification: A Journey of Professional Development.* Chicago, IL: Robin Fogarty & Associates.

Schlechty, Phillip C., (2002). *Working on the Work.* Jossey-Bass Publishers

Steffy, Wolfe, Pasch & Enz, (1999). *Lifecycle of the Career Teacher.* Corwin Press.

Thompson, Julia G., (2009). *The First Year Teacher's Checklist.* Jossey-Bass Publishers

Wong, Harry and Rosemary, (1998). *The First Days of School.* Wong Publications.

Bold entries are resources that you will find exceptionally helpful.

"THE LAST DAY…"

BY JERRY L. PARKS

AND SO, IT CAME TO PASS ON THE MORNING OF THE LAST DAY, THAT SOME BEHELD IN THE MIDST OF THEIR PEERS THE NOISE OF A FEARSOME AND GRIEVOUS TUMULT. AMONG THE MULTITUDES, AMIDST THE HOWLING AND SHUTTING OF BOOKS, WERE SEEN THOSE WHOSE QUEST FOR KNOWLEDGE LAY SCATTERED AND BROKEN UPON THE FLOOR OF OPPORTUNITY. AND FROM THEM WAS HEARD THE SOUND OF WAILING AND GNASHING OF TEETH—YEA, ALL HOPE WAS LOST…AND THEY WERE SORE AFRAID. THESE WERE THEY WHO HAD LEFT UNDONE THE THINGS WHICH THEY OUGHT TO HAVE DONE, AND HAD DONE NOT THE THINGS WHICH THEY OUGHT.

BUT LO, THERE WERE OTHERS—THOSE WHO HAD BEEN FOUND ABIDING IN THEIR ROOMS KEEPING WATCH OVER THEIR BOOKS BY NIGHT. THESE WERE THEY UPON WHOM OBEDIENT STUDY HAD BROUGHT TO PLENITUDE MUCH FRUIT. THESE AROSE IN PEACE, FOR THEY HAD PREPARED THEMSELVES, AND MADE STRAIGHT THE WAY OF KNOWLEDGE. PRAISE AND ADORATION SWELLED IN OBEISANCE AND ROSE IN EBULLIENT CHORUS TO THE GODS OF QUIZ AND REVIEW! AND THESE WERE CALLED THE WISE, BUT WERE KNOWN TO SOME AS 'THE BURNERS OF THE MIDNIGHT OIL,' BUT TO OTHERS AS 'THE CURVE WRECKERS.'

WITH LIFTED HANDS, AND FINGERS CALLUSED BY THE PURPOSEFUL ETCHING OF MANY NOTES UPON THEIR TABLETS, THE CHOSEN ONES STEPPED FORTH, BEING ANOINTED WITH THE OIL OF GLADNESS, AND FOREVER HUMBLED BY THE MERCIFUL ENDOWMENT OF THE GREAT SPIRIT KNOWN AS EXTRA CREDIT. BUT FOR THOSE WHO, IN HUBRIS, HAD STRADDLED THE LINE THAT LAY BETWIXT THE LAND OF ACADEMIC LIGHT AND FOOLDOM'S CHASM OF GREAT DARKNESS—THERE WAS ONLY SILENCE, AND THEIR HEART WAS HEAVY WITHIN THEM. THE FATE OF THE TREMBLING MULTITUDES WAS NOW LEFT TO BE WEIGHED UPON THE COLD AND IMPARTIAL SCALES OF MATHEMATICAL FORMULA, AND THEIR FUTURE ADRIFT UPON THE TIMELESS OCEAN OF WAITING AS THE ELDERS GATHERED TOGETHER TO MARK THE TERMINAL EDICT KNOWN AS 'THE FINAL EXAM.'

AND, LO, MANY WOULD BE FOUND WANTING. THEY HAD COME TO PASS, BUT MANY TO PASS OUT…AND SOME NOT TO PASS AT ALL. AND THE

MULTITUDE BEGAN TO REPENT OF THEIR WOEFUL HABITS OF STUDY, AND DREADED THEIR FATE. AT THE LAST, THERE WALKED AMONG THEM ONE KNOWN AS THE INSTRUCTOR, WHO TARRIED BUT A MOMENT. HE KNEW THAT MANY OF HIS TEACHINGS HAD FALLEN UPON FERTILE MINDS, WHILE OTHERS HAD FALLEN FLAT. HE TURNED FROM THEM SORROWFULLY, AND WENT UPON HIS WAY. AT THE LAST, AS SHADOWS LENGTHENED UPON THE LAST DAY, FATE DELIVERED ITS SENTENCE TO THE WAYWARD THRONGS. THE SILENCE OF THEIR SOLITUDE WAS BROKEN BY THE ANGUISHED TEARS OF RELIEF MOISTENING FURROWED BROWS, AS QUIVERING VOICES WERE HEARD TO PROCLAIM FROM THE VALLEY OF THE SHADOW OF DEATH: "…
I SHALL NOT PASS THIS WAY AGAIN."

Endnotes

[1] Armstrong, Coleen. (2009). *The Truth About Teaching*. Jossey-Bass Publishers

[2] *New York Times*, July 31, 2005

[3] Lemov, Doug. (2010). *Teaching Like a Champion*. Jossey-Bass Publishers

[4] Ornstein, A.C. *Knowledge as a Source of Change*: An Essay. NASSP Bulletin. Reston, VA, April, 1988, p. 73

[5] Ruggiero, V. (1988). *Teaching Thinking Across the Curriculum*. New York, NY: Harper and Row

[6] Averitt, Angela. (2008). *The Middle School Classroom: Prescription for Success*. BayWest Publishers

[7] Rosenthal, Robert & Jacobson, Lenore. (1992). *Pygmalion in the Classroom*. Expanded edition. New York: Irvington

[8] Jim Whitaker, *Safe Schools* consultant, Shelby Co. Schools, KY.

[9] Ebbinghaus, Hermann. (1885). *Memory: A Contribution to Experimental Psychology*. Teacher's College of New York

[10] Compiled from *The Classroom Teacher's Survival Guide*. Partin, Ronald L., (2009). Jossey-Bass Publishers

[11] ibid

[12] Payne, Ruby. (2005). *A Framework for Understating Poverty*. Aha Press, Inc.

[13] Forte, Imogene, and Schurr, Sandra. (1993). *The Definitive Middle School Guide*. Incentive Publications

[14] Ibid

[15] Parks, Jerry. (2007). *Help! My Child is Starting Middle School!* Weekly Reader Teacher's Press Publishers

[16] Forte, Imogene, and Schurr, Sandra. *Op cit*

[17] ibid

[18] Schlechty, Phillip C. (2002). *Working on the Work*. Jossey-Bass Publishers

CPSIA information can be obtained at www.ICGtesting.com
Printed in the USA
LVOW13s0852070813

346404LV00013B/483/P